R&D is War-
and I've Got the Scars to
Prove It

R&D is War-
and I've Got the Scars to Prove It

Clifford L. Spiro Ph.D

ISBN 978-1-300-41324-0

Acknowledgements

This book is dedicated to the hundreds of researchers, colleagues, and customers whom I have had the privilege to serve over my career. I hope in some small way, I made your business, your work, and your lives a little bit better. You have enriched me in countless ways for which I am eternally grateful.

Table of Contents

Introduction

Research and development, science and technology, innovation....call it what you like. R&D affects all of us, bringing us new and improved products and services, and propelling our markets and economies. Every time you walk down the rows of Home Depot or Wal*Mart, Sears, Walgreens and virtually every consumer or business-to-business enterprise, yes you are looking at products, but behind each product are countless, nameless individuals and their stories. No product made it to the shelves without a lot of work, and a lot of failures before it. I wrote this book for them and for you.

If you work in R&D, this book will amuse you and make you feel some comfort that others have travailed in anonymity just like you have, grinding away in the trenches of innovation—the labs and fabs that represent our second homes.

If you are in business, I hope this will enlighten you about the real world of advancing the needle of progress and why it costs so much for what always seems to be too slow, and with too little progress. And if you are a consumer of new products (and who isn't?) I hope you will find this to be a good, fun read and give you a new perspective as you stroll down the aisles of your favorite store.

Since 1973, I have been engaged in research and development or "R&D" for short. I did hands-on research as an undergraduate at Stanford, and as a graduate student at Caltech. For seven years at GE, I was fully engaged as an individual contributor, and for the next fifteen years at GE, I led progressively larger research teams, culminating in an assignment as General Manager of GE's halogen lamp engineering group with labs in Cleveland, Hungary, and

China. I left GE in 2001 to become VP of R&D at Nalco – a water, paper, and energy chemical company headquartered in Naperville, Illinois with labs in Sugar Land, Texas, Southampton and Aberdeen, UK, Leiden, Holland, Singapore, a small team in Spain, and as I was leaving, a facility we were getting underway in Helsinki. The company was owned by the French multinational utility Suez who quickly auctioned us off to private equity when they went low on cash; almost all of the officers got let go including me.

I next went to Cabot Microelectronics headquartered in Aurora, IL, and over the next 8 years, we would add labs in Geino, Japan, Hsinchu and then Tainan, Taiwan, Singapore, and Seoul, Korea. During this decade, I served on three industrial boards of directors of technology companies - Maxdem, Mississippi Polymer Technologies, and Strategic Diagnostics (SDIX). I also served on three academic boards at U. Chicago, Northwestern, and U. Arizona.

I list that brief bio only to illustrate that I have seen a lot of R&D. Naturally, over the years as a researcher and research-director, I have accumulated, first-hand, a number of R&D war stories- real life efforts to bring new science and technology to the marketplace. The stories in this book illustrate the dynamics of innovation, markets, people, processes, politics. They are mostly true, and mostly complete, though certain aspects have been disguised to protect the individuals, organizations, and company-proprietary information related to the stories. Where possible, I will highlight where I have taken liberties or felt compelled to leave certain pertinent information to the reader's imagination.

I am certain that everyone working in the advancement of technology has stories of his own, and I can guarantee that mine are neither unique, nor especially gory. But at least, I have a rather broad perspective on life in the slow lane, and I haven't really seen much comparable to the writing that follows. If you find this read valuable and have similar stories you'd like to share, please send them to me at cliff@cliffspiro.com. I hope to follow up with a series of "R&D Is War" stories that span your experiences as well as mine. I will certainly protect your anonymity and proprietary information per your instructions.

Finally, for those of you who don't know me personally, I have a wry sense of humor that often gets me into trouble. In this book, I like to poke fun at our Sales guys (order takers) and Finance guys (bean counters), among others. Please believe me that I have the highest respect for my colleagues in all functions. They are just as capable and dedicated as anyone in R&D, and I strongly value all functions- no organization can succeed without everyone across the organization doing their job well. R&D tends to be such an easy target that I couldn't resist taking a few shots back— forgive me.

It is my hope that you will enjoy the read and gain a new perspective on science and technology, invention and innovation, and the human and business sides of this hugely important segment of the workplace.

Chapter One

Sticky Business

In the late 1970's, America had a rude awakening from the OPEC oil embargo. Oil prices rose from $3.39 per barrel in 1970 to $37.42 per barrel in 1980 (www.inflationdata.com). If you are old enough, you might remember long lines at gas stations as supplies were rationed. For the first time, Americans were held hostage to forces in the Middle East, quite literally in Iran where fifty-two Americans were held prisoner for four hundred forty-four days by the Ayatollah, and figuratively as the American economy experienced stagflation at OPEC's hands. Stagflation is the combination of stagnation and inflation that resulted from skyrocketing energy costs. Stagflation destroyed American wealth by the bushel-full and eventually took down the Carter presidency. You may have doubts whether our policies and technologies have made things significantly better 40 years later, but for me personally, the energy crisis of the late 1970s served as the backdrop for commencing my career in R&D.

Fresh out of school with a PhD in chemistry from Caltech, in 1980, I joined GE's Corporate Research and Development laboratory in Schenectady, NY. My first assignment was rather ambiguous and open-ended—to simply learn about, and perform research on coal.

You probably know that the Chinese character for crisis includes characters for both risk and opportunity, and this is exactly how GE CEO Jack Welch and his predecessor Reg Jones saw the global energy situation. GE was heavily dependent on petrochemicals for its booming plastics business, and energy prices and efficiency served as a critical factor for driving technology leadership in its aircraft engines, power generation, diesel locomotive, lighting, and appliances businesses. So what did GE do? GE bought a coal company! I suppose even GE couldn't afford to buy a major oil company at the time, and GE already was a leader in the nuclear space, so coal would have to do.

Utah International was the mining concern that GE acquired back in 1976 for 2.2 billion dollars. The company owned several mines in the US, especially in the Navajo area around the Four-corners region of New Mexico, and in the Powder River Basin in Wyoming. It wasn't clear what R&D was actually needed for Utah International, but the company presumed that if we spent a couple billion of our shareholder's money, we ought to have a handful of technical specialists on hand. So the coal-science program was started at GE's central research labs with no loftier goals than to learn about coal, to find research topics of interest, and to be available as experts should we ever be needed. The ambiguity and open-ended assignment appealed to me and I became one of the foolish few to join.

The Coal Science Program at GE established research projects that included putting coal inside a medical CT scanner to study its "internal organs," analyzing the form and fate of sulfur and trace metals in coal using the powerful two-mile-long Stanford linear accelerator and synchrotron- the same one that was used to smash atoms and look for subatomic particles. We also had a project to turn coal into clean, combustible gases using novel catalysts. We modeled coal's molecular structure. In short—we learned about coal, became "experts," had some fun, wrote some good scientific papers, and didn't do a damn thing useful for Utah International or GE.

Utah International turned out to be such a bad fit for GE that in 1983, it was sold to a real mining company- Australia's Broken Hill Propriety—for a nominal profit, but really for an after-inflation and investment loss-- a billion or so as I recall. Chump change. The brass licked their wounds and we coal scientists were left holding an empty bag in R&D...or were we?

The Department of Energy Becomes My New Boss

The main mission of the US Department of Energy (DOE) at the time was to drive American energy independence, unlike today where the new mission of the US Department of Energy (DOE) is to drive American energy independence. Nice to know those folks in Washington are making enough progress that someday, they might even work themselves out of a job. But I digress....

America has abundant energy resources, mainly in the form of coal. Sadly, coal has a number of serious drawbacks. It is obviously a solid and most of our energy systems use liquid or gaseous fuels. And coal is dirty. Really dirty. It gives off soot, smoke, ash, oxides of nitrogen and sulfur that lead to acid rain, toxic mercury vapors, and even radioactive elements. And that is even before considering carbon dioxide and global warming issues.

The carbon in coal comes from the fossilized remains of primordial trees and plants. Coal also contains substantial mineral inclusions from the ancient soil- mostly clays, limestone, and sulfur-containing ores such as iron pyrite- so-called "fools gold" because of its brassy metallic luster.

The most common use of coal is to burn it as a solid in a boiler. The heat from combustion is used to raise steam which runs a steam turbine that in turn, generates electricity. The unburned minerals from the coal are captured as fly ash, and the gaseous sulfur oxides can be captured and cleaned at the boiler, though this is expensive. Moreover, this process is not terribly energy efficient and a large fraction of the energy gets lost as waste heat.

For years, scientists have known that burning coal directly in a gas turbine is potentially a more energy efficient process, augmented by the fact that the waste heat from the gas turbine can be re-used to run a steam turbine. This is called combined-cycle because it combines a gas turbine and a steam turbine. Right about the time that I was losing my *raison d'etre* – helping Utah International and ostensibly

GE, the US Department of Energy began a program to burn coal in a gas turbine. Naturally, they came to the four American turbine manufacturers for help, including GE. I was "volunteered" for the project, still as a loyal GE employee, but under contract to the DOE. Of course, most of the guys working at the DOE were ex-GE, but we don't need to go there.

To understand the project, let's first review my simple version of a gas turbine or jet engine. I think of a turbine as a fan, but run backwards. When you turn on your electric fan, electricity runs a motor, and the motor turns the blades of a fan. The fan blows air and keeps us cool. Pretty simple. Now imagine the process in reverse. Air is pushed backwards into a stationary fan, causing it to spin. If you then attach a generator to the fan running backwards, it produces electricity. Only rather than cool air blowing on a fan, in a real steam or gas turbine, respectively, it is steam from a boiler or hot combustion gases that push the blades around.

In the case of the coal-fired gas turbine, you could imagine that the hot gases from coal combustion do the trick to turn the blades and run the generators. You just blast the coal into a combustor that is attached to the gas turbine the same way a gas turbine works with liquid or gaseous petroleum. But there are a couple major issues- delivering the coal to the turbine in the right form, burning it really fast (think milliseconds), dealing with the ash and pollution.

The DOE knew this would be an engineering *tour de force*, and budgeted just under $100 million a year for several years, to be split among four contractors including GE obviously, each with unique approaches to solving the problems.

Our approach was to partner with a small company, Otisca Industries of Syracuse, which had been founded by an air-conditioning engineer, Clay Smith, and a surface chemist, Doug Keller. Together, they had come up with a way of "micronizing" coal by grinding it together with water in a very efficient process, and then cleaning most of the minerals out of the coal using "selective agglomeration." It is a simple process in concept. The coal is ground to a size of say 5 microns—something akin to the diameter of a human hair; think "powdered sugar." But the grinding takes place in water so you get a black muddy looking sludge known as coal-water-slurry.

Then you add the agglomerant- in this case liquid pentane—the flammable liquid you find in disposable cigarette lighters. Here is where it gets clever. You see, the hydrocarbon particles in the ground coal are attracted to the hydrocarbon liquid, and they all clump together like curds of black cottage cheese. But the minerals are more attracted to water, so they stay suspended as fine particles. It is easy to skim off the curds of the beneficiated coal and leave the minerals behind.

The Otisca process was often able to produce cleaned-coals with ash contents below 0.5%, whereas mined coal often contains 20, 30, or 40% non- combustible minerals to begin with. Now the process to burn coal in a turbine is going to be easy, we thought. Well....not so easy but we'll get there soon enough.

Otisca also found a way to recover all of the pentane and use it again, while redispersing the micronized coal back into water, and then into fifty-five gallon drums, where it was shipped to us to burn. The process was so clever that the Otisca guys built a huge pilot production plant using a refurbished cement factory outside of Syracuse, and were among the small company heroes reported in a Time Magazine cover story on "Chasing the American Dream," July 6, 1992.

GE's mechanical engineers then went to town, developing slurry distribution and handling systems, specialized fuel nozzles to atomize and spray the coal into the turbine combustor, and in short order, were able to successfully burn the coal to completion in time to run the turbine. Wow! So far, so good.

Now we get to the sticky problem of coal ash, pun intended. When the minerals in coal get hot enough, they melt and form a sticky, viscous glass called slag. Given that no two coals are identical in mineral content, these slags have a range of compositions and stickiness, but take my word for it— they were all plenty sticky under any reasonable gas turbine conditions. A test burn that might have been designed to run for hours never ran for more than seconds or maybe a couple minutes before the turbine blades got all gummed up and plugged. It might seem like 0.5% ash isn't very much, but the turbines were designed to run on ultra-pure fuels with trace metals at the parts-per-million level, so what we had on our hands was an unmitigated disaster. But at least, it wasn't unexpected by everyone including our sponsors at the DOE. After all, this had been tried before. But what could we do differently? "Your problem, Spiro—call me in the morning when you got it all worked out." Welcome to R&D.

We actually took the three logical approaches—clean the coal as much as possible using the new Otisca process while driving for even better cleaning processes; make the turbine as rugged as possible; and figure out ways to knock the ash off as it forms before it plugs or corrodes the metal. The turbine guys did a terrific job of making the turbine coal-worthy, and Otisca did a great job cleaning the coal, but it just wasn't enough.

Removing the melted ash and slag was tough. We had some experience removing ash when less dirty fuels than coal were used- for example burning the tarry residual oils left over after all the gasoline and chemicals are removed from petroleum. Here we literally put Brazil-nut shells (I kid you not) into the turbine every so often; they rattle around and knock the ash off of all the surfaces, and then whiz through the turbine and get harmlessly burned. But removing the coal-slag from the blades was nigh impossible; you could painstakingly chip little flakes off with a hammer and chisel, but basically, the stuff was truly permanently bonded to the blades. We needed something stronger than Brazil nuts— coconuts anyone? Anything we could think of was not even close to effective.

Here's where I came into the scene. Earlier, I mentioned that I had been studying coal minerals using synchrotron radiation at Stanford. I decided to try the same technique to study the slag that I had chiseled off of the surface of the turbine blades, in hopes that I might learn something useful.

Well— I did, or I obviously wouldn't be writing this story.

Using specialized X-ray absorption spectroscopy that is only possible at the accelerator, I found out that the typical slag was a glass containing potassium, aluminum and silicon, plus a host of other metals. One day, I was poring over several massive tomes entitled "Phase Diagrams For Ceramists," not exactly found on the NY Times best-seller list I know, but none-the- less interesting to me and a handful of nerds like me. Here I had a "Eureka" moment.

It occurred to me that, rather than removing more and more minerals to try to clean the coal as much as possible, what we really ought to do is to *add* more minerals, in particular, kaolin clay. Kaolin clay is used in numerous products such as a white filler in paper, and is mined and sold for dollars- per-ton. It is literally dirt cheap because it is dirt! Georgia dirt. But I reasoned that if we added enough of this clay to the coal-slurry, it would keep the ash from melting, so it wouldn't be sticky. And with a bit of luck, the new form of ash would remain fine enough to whiz along the streamlines of the turbine and never even hit the blades, let alone stick and corrode.

I would like to tell you that my powerful scientific reputation, deep intellect, and persuasive presentation skills combined to convince the power-to-be to try the experiment, but that wouldn't even be close to the truth. The fact is, I was a punk and we were simply desperate. But hey- desperation is often the strongest form of seduction, especially for engineering nerds, and it worked for me! So off I went to get a few drums of kaolin, added it to the slurry in the amounts I thought were needed to work, and we set up to run an experiment that we thought would last all of thirty seconds.

I should point out that running a real turbine experiment takes dozens of engineers and costs a bundle. We were using a turbine-simulator- a set of real turbine blades but that didn't actually rotate though they were aerodynamically true to the real thing. The blades just sat there. But the rest of the combustion system including a huge compressor the size of a municipal water tower, a combustion chamber inside an explosion-proof building, the slurry delivery systems—these all cost thousands of dollars per hour to operate, and took an army of engineers, too! But wasting big sums of money is the hallmark of research; at least that's what most CEO's think, anyway.

But let's get to the point. The experiment actually went beyond the minute, the hour, and went a full one-hundred hours before we depleted our entire supply of coal slurry. Our engineers calculated that the turbine was pretty clean from the pressure and temperature sensors they had all over the place, but only when we cracked open the turbine and saw gleaming silver blades, did we actually see and feel and believe it. It worked! It was glorious. It was certainly the most unforgettable and joyous moment of my young career. If engineers ever wanted to carry someone out of the lab on their shoulders, this was the time, though of course, it didn't happen. Let's not get ridiculous- these are still engineers and only resemble actual human beings.

The Department of Energy was overjoyed. This pixie-dust we added was white magic to them and I became "The Professor of Clinkerology." As a result of this project, the DOE decided to put all of their eggs in the GE basket, and cut way back on the other three suppliers' efforts. Our contract was extended, and my boss wrote me a bonus check for a thousand bucks to celebrate. And now, as I look out on the vast commercial enterprise of coal-fired gas turbines, it is with pride and joy and—oh wait! There are no commercial coal-fired gas turbines. What happened?

What happened was- the project was canceled, after all, and never saw the light of day. Economics is what happened. A funny thing about all these alternative energies- think Solyndra- they all say something like, "The price of oil is XXX dollars per barrel (say one hundred dollars for fun), and our breakeven point is one hundred twenty dollars a barrel." As oil inevitably goes up in price, the two cost lines will eclipse, and everyone will soon be using solar, nuclear, hydrothermal, bio---you name it. But of course, the price of oil is rather flexible, the new technology always costs more than was proposed to begin with, and anytime a new technology gets close, the oil price drops and we seem to forget all about the alternative and people like me and projects like mine become fodder for yesterday's news and tomorrow's books about why things didn't go the way we wanted.

But seriously-- how do we get out of this cycle?

Thomas Friedman, NY Times columnist and author, has proposed that the US government establish an energy floor price, say two hundred dollars a barrel. Any oil prices below this are to be taxed up to ensure that the customers will see no less than two hundred dollars a barrel. This gives the engineers and scientists and businessmen a clear, immutable target for alternatives; if they can just achieve a two hundred dollar cost, they are guaranteed to break even with oil. And sooner or later, they will. Anybody want to try proposing a one hundred per cent energy tax in Washington? So things never change and we are still under the thumb of the Middle East. And for now, no soap, and no coal-fired turbine. And I blew 7 years of my life on it. Down the toilet. Or not! As we will see in the next chapter, the science of clinkerology that led to the gleaming metal inside the turbine that at first overjoyed me and then crushed me, would turn out to be a silver lining and gold all wrapped up in one, and not once, but twice!

Lessons Learned

1.   Sometimes, a project that failed in the past can successfully be rekindled should the politics, economics, or technology shift. For example, politics and economics, along with improved alloys, turbine cooling, and coal-cleaning methods rekindled an interest in coal-fired turbines that had been dormant for decades. Someday, it may yet again roar its ugly head.

2.   Companies and countries sometimes invest in R&D based on faith that having experts will eventually pay off. In fact, as we will see over and over again,

despite extensive market analyses, financial projections, discounted cash flow analyses, competitive landscaping—virtually all investments in R&D are acts of faith.

3. There really are "Eureka" moments, where a new insight comes from the confluence of knowledge, observation, insight, and luck. In this case, the breakthrough came from the new concept that, rather than cleaning the coal, making it dirtier in just the right way might make a difference.

4. Solving the technical barriers does not ensure commercial success.

Chapter Two

A Brick Is a Terrible Thing to Waste

Networking is a reasonably modern term, thanks to Facebook® and Linked-in®, but a careful study back in the 1980s of uber-successful researchers at Bell Labs, and published in the Harvard Business Review, demonstrated that the cream of the Bell Labs R&D guys were the ones who networked the best. Now to put things in perspective, just making it to Bell Labs as a researcher is the equivalent of playing for the Yankees. So we are talking about some seriously exclusive company.

I can't say why, but I have always been a networker. Maybe it is because so many of us in R&D are such antisocial nerds that I just appear to be highly connected, but compared to the schmoozers in Sales or Marketing, I am probably a social slouch. Why am I picturing my entire Sales Department's heads bobbing in unison?

In any case, my network was the reason my good friend, Tom Guggenheim called me up out of the blue to share a problem his group in GE Plastics was having; not to ask for help per se', but because I knew so many odd people, surely I could identify one of them who could help him. And given the eclectic nature of coal, I had indeed truly been thrust in contact with an odd assortment. After all, coal is a fuel, a fossil, a plastic, a mineral, a pollutant. In my seven years with coal, I had encountered a broad mix of chemists, biologists, engineers, applied physicists, (unapplied physicists?), ceramists, metallurgists, mechanical engineers, environmental engineers and the like.

To Tom's surprise, I told him, "I can solve your problem!" Ahh, don't you love the hubris of youth?

GE Plastics had a new plastic resin called Ultem® that was really amazing, keeping its strength at unusually high temperatures-- enough to cook with or use under the hood of a car, for example. But they were having a teensy problem with their production process. One of the waste streams in their manufacturing process contained an extremely small concentration of a molecule that was considered to be a suspect teratogen. What that means to normal human beings is that one of the chemical byproducts from the overall set of chemical reactions to produce Ultem® kind of looked like something that was occasionally found to cause birth defects, so GE Plastics needed to burn the waste to be on the safe side. No big deal, right? Wrong!

Unfortunately, the waste stream containing the suspect teratogen was also extremely corrosive because it contained a large concentration of caustic soda which was necessary to manufacture the resin. Caustic soda is a *bona fide* nasty chemical that you don't really want to come in contact with- it will basically burn all the flesh off of you in no time. It's what the bone guys use to do just that. But in the case of GE Plastics, it was quite literally dissolving the lining inside of the incinerator—9 inches of fire brick spalling off, often in less than a month.

When they designed and constructed the incinerator, it was sized to handle twice as much waste as they were planning on producing. The reason they built it so large was in case the business was a big success, in which case they could double the output of the plant but not have to build another incinerator. A new incinerator would require a long and painful permitting process, so they over-designed it. But in reality, by the time Tom called me, it was actually only handling less than half of their waste, and that with great difficulty.

Several times during the period when the incinerator was up and running, a huge chunk of bricks a few feet wide would break off and plug the furnace, and the outer steel shell would glow red-hot. This would inevitably happen at 3

AM, during your child's birthday party, or the start of the fourth quarter of the Super Bowl. They would emergency-shut the thing down, cool it for a day or two, and then clean away the broken bricks and patch the hole. Finally after thirty or forty-five days of intermittent operation, they would just give up, remove all the brick, replace it with something new, and start over. Think weeks and hundreds of thousands of dollars a pop.

In order to temporarily maintain production while the incinerator was down, GE Plastics rented huge oil storage tanks just up the road overlooking the Ohio River, and in a couple of years, they had filled them to the gills with this caustic and potentially teratogenic waste. How would you like to be plant manager if that tank gave out? What a nightmare. And even more immediately, they had completely run out of storage space for their waste, and the business president refused to allow them to rent another tank.

So they ran the plastics production process for a while, burning the waste that they could, and then when the incinerator shut down, so did the Ultem® process. We call this "campaigning" the reactors, and it is a horrible way to run a chemical business. The right way is to get the process running, then work like hell to tweak the process to run at its absolute best, and then keep it there for as long as you can, augmented by extensive prayer sessions. Startups and shut-downs are extremely difficult, causing a lot of waste and problems, and can even be dangerous. But the business president was clear—fix the problem or shut it down.

Tom and his associates did what anyone would do in their shoes- they called vendors and asked for their help, then consultants, then professors, and finally the most expensive experts in the world (see Chapter Four) at Corporate R&D in Schenectady. It was already two years after those measures failed to achieve appreciable progress, and they were up the proverbial creek without a paddle, when Tom called me and asked for help.

Having solved the problem of coal slag sticking to turbines, as we saw in Chapter One, I had an ace in the hole—if adding clay or some other cheap dirt worked for turbines, it would work for incinerators, or so I reasoned. Surely all I would need to do was find something to add to the waste stream that would keep the brick from corroding. Kaolin clay? Isn't ignorance bliss?

So here was the plan. Tom sent me several gallons of waste. One of my associates designed a rotary kiln- a mini version of the incinerator. I ordered a suite of bricks and ceramics and cements and the guys in the furnace shop made up dozens of experimental bricks. My plan was to analyze the byproducts from the combustion process just like I had with the coal slag, then look at my trusty "Phase Diagrams for Ceramists," figure out what to add, and then prepare for my victory dance. I chose several bricks to evaluate because I wanted to start with something relatively easy to modify, and I didn't know which would be the best to begin with.

Our first few test bricks were absolutely disintegrated. Things were looking rather grim. But for some reason, undoubtedly divine intervention, test brick number eight didn't react when we put it in the kiln with the waste. It just sat there and looked pretty much like it had when we started the test! Curious? Yes. But who cared? I told Tom to stop the presses, line the incinerator with brick number eight, and their problems would be solved. And you know, Tom and a very courageous manufacturing manager, Dave Mongilio, did exactly that. Again— was this from their confidence and belief and trust of a respected researcher with detailed analyses, scientific data, impeccable credentials? Nope- once again our good friend "desperation" worked for me. And it worked for the folks at Ultem® as well. Beautifully, in fact.

Within a year, they had not needed to replace any of the bricks, had no annoying shutdowns, had burned all their waste without a problem, and had completely drained the waste storage tanks. I believe that one zone of the furnace lasted over three years and for all I know, some of the original bricks may still be in there! We estimated that the value of plant uptime, incinerator material and labor costs, and lower operating costs benefited GE to the tune of 9 figures. And eliminating the risks of an environmental disaster? Priceless!

We never actually figured out why the brick worked so well, though after the fact I could hand-wave my way to an explanation involving brick structure and chemistry that was probably close to the truth, but who cared? It worked, and that was the key, even though we got lucky. This time I didn't get a check for my nine figures of benefit to GE, but I did get a nice trophy that says "Plastics Team of The Year" that I may still have, somewhere in a cardboard box in my basement next to my third-place golf-league trophy from 2004 and my certificate for completing six-sigma-green-belt training in 1996. Who needs money, anyway, as long as you have great stories and plastic bling? True?

Sadly, there was an interesting twist to this story. At the time, GE's central research was largely funded by contracts with the businesses. For example, GE Plastics paid for my short project with the bricks. In our system, a researcher was mainly evaluated on the money he brought in to the research center, as I'll discuss in Chapter Four. The presumption was that, if you were doing good and important work, the best way to know this was by the dollars of research funds you brought in. Universities work the same way.

It turns out that my premature solution to the failing brick problem cut the gravy train off. Obviously, there was no longer the need to fund a project that was already solved. I essentially killed the goose that laid the golden egg and some of the bean counters at the research center were not too happy about that. Oh well. That's their problem, not mine.

Lessons Learned

1.   Again we see that desperation is really the mother of invention, not mere necessity.

2.   If something worked once, see where else it might work. In this case, the concept of changing slag chemistry through the addition of minerals was learned in the coal-fired turbine project, and would be applied here. I can't say it worked here—we never got that far, but it might have.

3.   In sales, they say, "When you have made the sale, stop talking." In R&D, when you have solved the problem, stop working.

4.   Always seek the fastest, simplest solution to a problem.

5.   Networking in science is just as important as networking in business. Especially with the explosion and divergence of knowledge, collecting a bunch of smart friends is a real differentiator. But left-brained scientists don't tend to naturally network like you might find among sales and market folks, so this behavior is more of an exception than a rule.

6.   Even if you don't know the technology of a problem well, try your ideas in the lab. Sometimes, just trying something, anything—and making observations and quick adjustments—is better than fretting in the library over finding the perfect solution. Look where that led in this case; a business literally saved and mostly serendipitously. Coming at a problem from unique perspectives can really bear fruit.

Chapter Three

A Threepeat!

This is a short chapter, not because it isn't interesting, but because the projects were classified. The technology involved the invisible world of low observables, "LO" to the cognoscenti and "stealth" to most of us.

The concepts of stealth are well-known and no longer classified. Through a combination of shape (think about the flying wedge that comprises the B2 bomber) and materials, radiation used to sense the object gets absorbed instead of reflected back to the detector.

For radar absorption, the coatings contain microscopic particles of ferrous metals such as iron, cobalt, and nickel. You may know that radar uses radio-waves which are like visible and ultraviolet and infrared light, all of which are forms of what is called electromagnetic radiation. In all electromagnetic radiation including radar, there are oscillating magnetic and electric fields. The assembly of dispersed magnetic particles in stealth works like a swarm of bees to absorb the just a small fraction of the magnetic portion of the radar waves. One nice thing about stealth— you don't need to absorb everything; if just one component gets absorbed, then the detector sitting on the enemy's plane is blinded.

One problem with radar-absorbing-materials (RAM) is that finely divided metal particles burn. In fact, they burn like hell! I know you have played with a sparkler at some point in your life, those sticks that look like a giant metal Q-Tip. Sparklers are made up of exactly the same stuff that makes up RAM- finely divided ferrous metals. Funny thing—the Air

Force is not exactly keen about their planes going up in a sparkle, and even the worst air force in the world wouldn't have much trouble spotting a giant flash bang in the sky. So GE developed a way to make sure that didn't happen. For the record, I had nothing to do with that part of the process. The guys who developed the way to protect the RAM from burning did a remarkably good job, as we'll see later.

But—we did have a slight problem; getting it to stick to a jet engine. Military jet engines get very hot very fast, especially during afterburner at launch and take-off. Most materials expand and contract with each temperature cycle, and it is extremely difficult to find two or three materials to expand and contract at exactly the same rate. So whatever we have that is stealthy and whatever is holding it onto the plane are likely to be very different from the engine materials themselves. Indeed this stuff had a serious propensity to fall off. My mission was to get the stuff to stick, and if I failed, my boss would disavow all knowledge of me and the program.

I bet some of you by now have guessed what I did to solve this problem. Remember that lousy coal-ash from chapter one that stuck to everything? You guessed it- I found out what was in that coal slag that made it so sticky, and made up a synthetic version. We did the lab tests known as high-cycle fatigue and it passed with flying feathers. After that, I have no idea if it actually went into production. The secret world is a black hole and the less you know, the better.

Having solved the issue of high temperature adhesion, I faced an even more fun problem with stealth materials. I told you the guys did a great job making this stuff indestructible. That should be a good thing, but after a while, all the scraps from the process started accumulating, and as long as they absorbed radar, the government considered them classified at the time. So what started as a small safe of secret stuff eventually became a large warehouse filled with stealth scrap, and the building was sealed and guarded twenty-four/seven by a crew of large, well-armed and well-paid men who lacked a sense of humor. Because I was one of the few guys that held the right "Special-Need-To-Know" security clearance, I was given the juicy task of finding a way to destroy the waste. As a chemist, this should have been easy, but all the usual stuff- heat, radiation, and harsh chemicals didn't do the job.

I should have given up, but then I had a thought...If this stuff is so indestructible, why don't we just grind it up and recycle it? Instead of accumulating and storing waste, or going to heroic and expensive measures to destroy it, why not just clean it up, mix it with some virgin materials, and sell it? That little project paid off big!

The recycled stealth materials sold for something like a hundred dollars a pound, so our little effort to recycle the waste not only killed two birds with one stone, but added seven figures to the company bottom line. Granted that this isn't big money to a hundred billion dollar company, but each person in R&D costs a lot—probably two hundred fifty thousand a year for salary, overhead, materials, and support. Each year, somebody from Finance invariably asks, "What did we get from paying that Spiro character all that money?" and at least back in the early eighties, I had an answer. Of course, my first answer was always, "What do we get from paying you Finance guys all that money?" But they would just look back at me like chickens watching card tricks, and then ask their question again.

I should say that working on classified projects was great. For one thing, there were no project reviews because nobody was cleared to hear about the projects except the people working on them themselves. Plus we had a great secret lab that nobody could enter but me and my colleague and one guy from Security, so that if we wanted to, we could keep our poker winnings, cigars, and naughty pictures safely on the lab bench and away from our wives, not that we were so inclined, of course. But at least, it was certainly a nice, quiet space to rest...I mean work.

Lessons Learned

1. Once again, transferring technology and not reinventing the wheel was the key to success—in this case, knowing that some coal ash substance

was glue for turbines would also be glue for jet engines.

2.   Techies really do grow in value with time and experience, and investing in their accumulation of knowledge pays off in unexpected and unpredictable ways.

3.   It is nice when you can justify your existence by having a financial impact much greater than your costs, in any field of course, but especially in R&D where the payoffs may not be fast or obvious. I remember when I first told John Bercaw, a professor at Caltech, that I was going to GE. He said, "You'll be real happy there once you make them a million dollars."

4.   Instead of solving a problem that you are assigned such as "Dispose of this waste," there may be a better solution such as "Re-use this waste for its primary or secondary purpose." It is always good to challenge the original task goals to see if there are better ones.

5.   Sometimes, solving one problem creates a new problem. By making the stealth materials "indestructible," we created the problem of storing it securely. This is also known as "job security" for scientists.

Chapter Four

Show Me the Money

I have already alluded to the money needed to do research, but let's take a hard look now at the challenges of funding research, and then put it mostly behind us.

Research is not cheap. The total domestic spend on all research is estimated to be 1.2 trillion dollars according to Battelle, about a third of that which is spent worldwide. Those are some pretty big numbers, but not when you think of all the things that go into the care and feeding of a typical research project. Of course, we have the researcher's salary which is around a hundred grand a year these days but which can vary from a few thousand dollars for an undergraduate or technician in a low cost country, to a few hundred thousand for a superstar. Let's then add overhead which includes benefits, facilities such as labs, offices, the library, storeroom, heating and ventilation, management, patent attorneys and on and on. Figure about two hundred fifty per cent of actual overhead for each scientist. Then there are additional direct project expenses including materials, equipment, technicians and associates, stuff we break and consume, books and articles we need to read, travel to important scientific meetings in Hawaii and Las Vegas, and bottomless cups of coffee. The care and feeding of a researcher is a costly venture indeed.

Now multiply this by the tens of thousands of researchers throughout the world, and you can see why the numbers in paragraph one are so big.

There are endless debates over whether the benefits of R&D surpass the costs, and often investments in individual research projects do indeed fall short, especially when looked at on a granular basis. But a few especially big hits, and a lot of incremental projects really do pay off. And as we have already seen, what failed once, may turn out to be a big breakthrough later when the lessons-learned are applied differently. Obviously, the coal-fired turbine project in chapter one failed because empirically, there simply are no commercial coal-fired turbines; but the twenty thousand dollars spent on the Ultem® Bricks project in Chapter Two paid off in nine figures by applying the lessons learned from the turbine. In aggregate, the coal-fired turbine project was a huge success when considering the spinoffs it led to. But try putting that in a spreadsheet.

Virtually all human progress, the growth of the world product, and accumulated world wealth came out of some innovation somewhere. A huge portion of any organization's market cap is comprised of projected future earnings from as-yet undeveloped innovations and new products. It may come as little solace to the individual business segment that is funding a particular project that fails to achieve the desired results, that somewhere else in the world, a similar competitive team probably will succeed. But as a society, there is no doubt, at least to me, that investment in technology has paid off big, and will continue to do so. Pity the poor chump who backed a loser, as most projects turn out to be.

So let's get back to understanding the care and feeding of your garden variety research program.

Most of the universities get their money from the government. The big-hitting funding agencies include the National Institute of Health, the Defense Department, Energy, Commerce, Homeland Security and so on. Typically, individual professors will write grant proposals to the various organizations-projects that are loosely matched to the missions of the respective agencies. Proposals are often peer-reviewed which makes the funding a bit of an old-boy network in which senior professors who have spawned junior professors form a mutual admiration society and support each other's grant proposals, tenure and award nominations, and publications. Grants range from tens of thousands of dollars to millions for especially large projects.

Some universities, national labs, and major research institutions such as Fermilab or the Stanford Linear Accelerator Center will apply for large block grants that will fund several research teams. And smaller centers of excellence will get multi-year grants that support a handful of research teams. For example, I sat on review boards at U. Chicago's Materials Research Science and Engineering Center (MRSEC) and U. Arizona's Center for the Environmentally Benign Processing of Semiconductors both of which received multiyear block grants in the millions of dollars, and supported five to twenty major projects. Eventually, the funds are disbursed and trickle into individual professors and graduate students' budgets, of course after the institutions take a big cut to pay for their overhead.

The grant-chasing process is perhaps the primary activity of major research universities and their staffs, distantly followed in importance by actually performing the research, and finally, by teaching. Professors who successfully raise a lot of money are prized by their institutions, and ones who don't generate big bucks quickly end up in third or fourth tier colleges, teaching and eking out small undergraduate research projects that eventually lead to minor publications. It is a sad fall from grace for the professor who can't feed his team.

In industry, funding R&D is a different beast.

When I first started at GE, it was pretty simple. We basically got all of our money from the headquarters in a lump sum, with some additional funds coming from direct government contracts and government kick-backs. Each of the businesses turned over their revenues and profits to the corporation, who in turn distributed them among shareholders, employees, and reinvestment in the business including new plants and equipment, and of course, R&D. Life was good. Each year we would tell our story to our bosses, who would condense them into one big story that would get told at headquarters. I presume that there was the usual mix of hubris, sandbagging, padding, hyperbole, whining, and begging—and in the end, GE paid the bills. If the company felt we were spending too much, we would contract mainly through attrition, and if the company wanted to do more research, we would grow. Year-to-year changes were in the sub-ten-per cent- barely noticeable at the bench. And certainly, fundraising was not a major activity in my early years.

I mentioned government kickbacks a few paragraphs ago. Back in the 80's, any large defense contractor almost automatically received lump sums in proportion to the government spend, presumably to do research in the national need. GE was a big defense contractor so we got a lot of money. I don't exactly know how much we got back in the early 1980's, but my recollection was that about fifteen-to-twenty per cent of our budget came from these Industrial Research and Development (IRD) funds. Of course, a large annual proposal and accounting was required to show that the Defense Department was getting lots of good stuff for their buck, and many of us had to write a paragraph about our particular projects to show how the country benefited. But all in all, it was easy money.

A small fraction of our funding came from the US government through a variety of bid-and-proposal activities. Often an agency such as the DoE or DoD/DARPA (Defense Advanced Research Procurement Agency) would publish a request for proposal (RFP) or Broad Agency Announcement (BAA) asking for proposals. Prior to these publications, GE and most every other company in search of funding would spend a lot of time with the agencies and their program managers to plant seeds of what we wanted to do, and to find out what their pet projects were going to be. So that by the time a BAA or RFP was published, it was pretty clear who was going to get funded.

None the less, writing these proposals was an ordeal. A grant proposal would generally consist of three large books each a hundred-plus pages which included descriptions of people, facilities, background, and eventually a statement of work. And then there was the small matter of financials, in which virtually every cost was itemized. It would take the principal investigator (PI) and a team from R&D and procurement and government relations, a solid month to write and publish these proposals. Over the years, I was PI on twelve major grants that brought in fifty-one million dollars. And these grants not only paid for the research, but also the two hundred fifty per cent overhead that helped cover our facility and utility costs, and often included a small fee, maybe seven per cent, which was sort of profit, but basically went back to the company to help fund the writing of additional proposals.

And though we were a private corporation, I really had no problem seeking, receiving, and spending the taxpayers' dollars on research because it truly was in the national interest. And if you are bringing in money to pay for some or all of your research, the company was more than happy to keep you around since you weren't costing them anything; you were helping them pay the rent; and there was always the remote possibility that someone might get educated or even come up with something useful. Nice.

Around 1983 or 1984, our world got upended by Walt Robb, our new Senior VP of R&D and GE's Chief Technology Officer. Walt is a fabulous guy— Illinois PhD in Chem E and a brilliant researcher in his own right-- who entered management relatively late in his career and enjoyed a spectacular rise through several of our businesses, culminating as CEO of GE Medical Systems. At Med Systems, Walt transformed what had been an obscure X-Ray tube business into a multi-billion-dollar medical imaging behemoth, with leading edge modalities in X-Ray Computed Tomography (CT), Magnetic Resonance Imaging (MRI), ultrasound imaging, and Positron-Emission-Tomography (PET) for brain scanning. Entering his last few years at GE, Walt would transform GE's R&D- quickly, boldly, and simply.

By the time Walt took over Corporate Research and Development (CRD), he had been well-steeped in the lore at headquarters that CRD was largely irrelevant, working on "Science Projects" for the edification and amusement of the scientists, but of little value to the businesses. And the business CEO's, including Walt, resented the large corporate assessment that went into central research.

In one decisive, fell swoop, Walt changed all of that. From the moment that Walt took over, researchers would no longer get a blank check from headquarters, but would need to get funds directly from the businesses, on a project-by-project basis, and therefore, ostensibly only work on projects that mattered to the sponsors. The businesses were under no official compulsion to fund CRD, though presumably, if they cut back too much in order to achieve their short-term earnings, Walt would whisper to Jack Welch, GE's legendary CEO, and Jack would "gently" speak with the business president, and some of their funds might get loosened up after all for CRD. Or so rumor would have it. But basically, the businesses were calling the shots and the researchers needed to contract with them or starve.

The angst with Walt's arrival at CRD, and especially his funding proclamation, was palpable. There was so much vitriol about abandoning our future and working only on short term tweaks and being dependent on the businesses and having to chase funding—that many terrific researchers actually quit and went to the university. Of course, raising money there is really much harder, so the joke was on them.

I was young and foolish enough to stick around. Plus, I was already mostly funded by the US Department of Energy, so the change had no immediate effect on me.

After a couple years, I became a Program Manager which is the first managerial level at CRD, requiring a combination of hands-on research, leading a small team, and primarily- raising money for our researchers. So I spent a lot of time with our businesses and business leaders, many of whom held a long-standing resentment and animosity toward funding research at CRD rather than in their own local and dedicated labs. Certainly this was due to the distance factor—if you are a business GM and your researchers are just down the hall, it is easy to tell them what to do and hold them accountable; less so if your team is in Schenectady, NY and reports up through Corporate. But this was only one part of the issue. The other was cost.

If a business manager wanted to pay for a researcher in his facility, he would just pay for his salary and expenses. You see, the overhead – buildings, equipment, maintenance—were already borne by the businesses. But if they hired a researcher at CRD, they would be charged the full freight—salary, benefits, direct costs, and the two hundred fifty per cent overhead on top. CRD researchers were not paid substantially more than the guys in the business, and the real overhead was not any higher because a lab is a lab whether it is in Cleveland or Schenectady, but to the GM writing the check, he could really hire three engineers in Cleveland for one in Schenectady. A few of the GM's understood that this was just bad accounting, but it didn't really matter.

This made my job very hard. I had to overcome this huge cost differential. I explained this very succinctly to Walt, and only wanted fair and balanced accounting lest the businesses make a sub-optimal decision. For example, maybe they could hire a truly world-class metallurgist at CRD for a quarter million dollars, or they could hire an OK metallurgist in Cincinnati or Milwaukee or Erie where they had their own labs, for maybe eighty thousand dollars. Often they spent the eighty thousand and got much less brainpower. For big GE, it was really two-hundred fifty thousand dollars no matter where the guy sat, but for the GM, it was a three-for-one mismatch. I believed this poor accounting led to bad decisions.

Walt was nonplused though he completely grasped my argument and concern. His response was, "Hey if your guys aren't three times as good as theirs, you don't deserve to be here." Walt did not pull any punches.

And of course, he was right.

The next several years, as a Program Manager, I travelled from business to business, trying to understand their problems and match my group's capabilities to their needs. I was as much in Sales as I was in R&D. But it was really a good opportunity for me. My group was in advanced materials and coatings, especially high performance metallurgical and ceramic coatings. These are applied to jet engines, gas turbines, stealth, medical devices such as X-Ray tubes and MRI magnets, abrasives and wear surfaces, appliances, and in all sorts of processes. I had the unique privilege of going from business to business and hearing about their dirty linen, and then working with my team, posing solutions or at least, research that would lead to solutions. It was great-- I learned so much, and met some fantastic people.

My fundraising at CRD consisted of three prongs—get some of the residual corporate money which constituted about a fourth of our overall budget; go for government contracts; and raise money through our businesses. Some of the other Program Managers were one-trick ponies- relying entirely on one business such as GE Plastics or GE Aircraft or GE Lighting. If the individual business caught a cold one year, their corresponding programs at CRD caught pneumonia. I at least had lots of ways to find money. And my team was strong enough to make this work, albeit with months of angst as we rounded through the budgeting annual biorhythms.

When I finally left CRD and transferred to GE Silicones (Chapter Seven), the shoe was sort of on the other foot as I got to determine how much funding to give to CRD. But I would still have to beg, borrow, and steal that money from the Silicones business managers, anyway. At least my budget was largely covered by the business teams. But even at Silicones, and soon enough from GE Lighting, I had to compete with other research groups, and even other departments such as Marketing or Manufacturing for scarce resources.

At GE Lighting, every project was put on a vast spreadsheet, and included the cost, benefit, timing, and discounted rate of return or DCRR. For the finance guys, this is basic stuff, but for the rest of us, DCRR is basically a measure of how fast and how much the project will pay for itself compared to just leaving the money in the bank. We would each estimate our several projects' returns along with probability of success, and then rack and stack them. Cost reductions were compared equally with quality improvements, equipment investments, safety, marketing programs, and new products of all sorts. Once the spreadsheet was rolled up, we got to change our numbers to try to exceed the cutoff point. But of course, everyone else was flexing their numbers too. Eventually, you couldn't shift things any more, and the project deck was set in stone.

Now anyone who has ever done a DCRR calculation knows that these are about as loose as a goose. You just need to change the cost, price, start date, end date, volume, foreign exchange rate—you name it. Manipulating the numbers was a piece of cake, and it was also a silly exercise. In the end, the projects for manufacturing cost reductions always won because they were implemented immediately, and had a high degree of certainty to work. Plus, the Manufacturing VP, Joe Barranco, seemed to have Finance in his pocket. It is not surprising that by focusing almost entirely on cost, GE Lighting eventually lost its innovation edge, forcing Jack Welch to step in and stop the nonsense, as we'll hear about in Chapter Fourteen. But in the interim, whole bunches of people played these financial games that amounted to little more than a waste of time.

When I finally left GE in 2001 and moved first to Nalco/Suez, I encountered a whole new budget and planning process designed and implemented by the French! Now the French are an interesting lot, as has been written about in a fantastically insightful article "The Making of a French Manager" published in the July, 1991 Harvard Business Review. In the French system, logic and self-consistency are paramount. Results? Not so important as long as you had a good enough plan. I think the whole country of France pretty much operates the same way.

The French planning system was so convoluted that I will devote another chapter to it later (Chapter Eighteen).

Finally at Cabot Microelectronics, I encountered a pretty darn reasonable budget and funding process. We also put together annually a long-range-plan (LRP) that would project incomes and expenses out a few years, and it was just as much science-fiction as we had with Suez, but at least everyone knew it, though we tried to make the underlying strategic discussions rich and thoughtful. When the budget finally came from the Board of Directors and the CEO, each VP was given a target budget for them to try and achieve. Then there was a series of sixteen-hour discussions between Finance and each department VP to see just how each group would make their budget. I always was well-prepared, having gone to each of my leaders to pre-negotiate their budgets so that the totals would add up.

Then when the Finance folks met with me, I would always present a number that was actually less than they proposed! That always made the discussions go well from the start. And from there, we would work together to find even more money to give back. After all, I understood that we were in business to make money, and controlling costs was in everyone's best interest. But I also had a couple aces in the hole. For one thing, I always pushed hard to manage costs as I'll discuss in Chapter Twenty-three, and it became engrained in R&D's culture. Normally we would find two or three million dollars of savings each year, which was pretty big considering we had a fifty million dollar budget to begin with. Plus the Finance department would always budget for a full head count, but people were constantly leaving or transferring, and hiring backfills always took time. Generally if they budgeted for two hundred employees in R&D, we might actually never have more than one hundred ninety or one hundred ninety-five because of the hiring lag. This also saved a lot of money. Sure my leaders would panic when their budgets got cut, but we never actually ran out or over-ran. Plus, by going to Finance proactively and looking for even more cuts than they proposed, whenever we had a new, special project that came along mid-year, we had so much credibility by earnestly trying to manage our costs, that they always supported the effort to free up additional funds.

And as my boss at CRD once told me, nobody ever got fired for missing their budget as long as they deliver the goods. Good advice.

Lessons Learned

1. The money to do research is big, and finding it is a major task for everyone along the food chain. All researchers have to become salesmen by necessity. For a large fraction of the best and brightest, fund-raising becomes all-encompassing, with the "doing" often subjugated in effort and importance.

2. Funding research may seem like an elaborate financial dance, replete with DCRR calculations and elaborate customer plans and timing. But in fact, this is all a shameless ruse designed to allow the people who are paying the bills to feel that the costs are justified. However, R&D really is an act of faith, something that the sponsors fully grasp, fear, and resent. Fortunately, the researchers occasionally deliver something useful, though often unintended, and big enough to make the gamble worth it. And not funding the future is a sure way to quickly go out of business.

3. The elaborate money dance to fund R&D may seem like a colossal waste of time, but if it really brings sharp thinking to real problems, and engages customers with researchers, along with sales, marketing, finance and operations, this is intrinsically valuable, ensuring that the organization is all working together and on the same page, and that no "Science Projects" exist for the enjoyment of the researchers.

4. If you want to inflame anyone in R&D, just say that they are working on science projects, presumably for their own amusement. However be prepared for them to leave and go work for your competition, taking all of your secrets and accumulated knowledge with them. You really have invested millions in their training so I hope the momentary satisfaction you got out of suggesting that your

techies were irrelevant, and the amusement from their angry response was worth it. But that's OK— we researchers know that everyone in Sales is an order-taker while we do the heavy lifting, and that everyone in Finance is a bean-counter.

Chapter Five

Turning Trapezoids into Squares

Around this time in my career, GE bought a small ceramics company from 3M and aptly named it GE Ceramics. I imagine someone on Madison Avenue made a million bucks coming up with that moniker....do I sound bitter? 3M had actually bought the company from American Lava who apparently was struggling with it at the time; 3M struggled and sold it to GE; GE struggled and eventually sold it to Coors, and I have no idea if the Laurens, SC and Chattanooga, TN company is still around. In any case, I got sucked into it for a while.

Before I get into the meat-and-potatoes of the story, there is an interesting prelude I want to share. Corporate R&D has a famous and extensive Ceramics Research Department, replete with several members of the prestigious National Academy of Engineering. It was well-understood that the Ceramics Department would take the lead in integrating the new business group and augmenting its technology. My group, on the other hand, was made up of mainly mechanical engineers. When the acquisition was completed, my bosses sent me down to visit the new facilities on a fact- finding mission ostensibly to see if there was a way we could help the new business in ways outside of the Ceramics Department scope. Of course, in reality, they were looking for a new source of research funds *a la* Chapter Four. In any event, I got a nice boondoggle to Chattanooga, TN and Laurens, SC.

After a couple days, I returned home with a reasonable understanding of the processes and issues in the new enterprise. My boss called me up and invited me over to give a debrief on what I had learned.

Expecting just one or two people, I made no formal preparation—just a few hand notes and sketches. As Joan Rivers would say, "Can we talk?" I walked into my boss's office and he motioned me to the Combustion Building main conference room, which I observed was completely filled with our entire department of about forty engineers! I tried to remember from my "Extemporaneous Speaking" class what was the proper procedure on how to cover a large brown spot in my pants.

Actually, once I got started, just talking as if I was just hanging around the coffeepot with my buddies, the discussion went great! There was lots of interchange, good questions and discussion, and we all earnestly were looking for issues and opportunities. Over the next thirty years or so, I would give around a hundred technical and business presentations each year to all sorts of audiences ranging from scientists at conferences, all-employee meetings, high school teachers, college classes, politicians and government officials, boards of directors, investors-- and yet I recall this one as being the tops. I tend to believe that people communicate best when they are just being themselves, and that the more formal the presentation and the more preparation—the further it gets from being who the speaker is and what he wants to accomplish. It was certainly an interesting lesson for me.

Now back to the technology.

GE Ceramics made multilayer ceramic chip carriers. These are little tiny ceramic squares about a centimeter in length and width and a few millimeters thick. Computer chips sit on, or inside of, square cavities on the surface. Usually made of plastics, the ceramic versions of chip carriers are used for heavy duty applications in trucks and planes, military and aerospace, and radiation-hard environments.

What made our chip carriers complicated and higher value, was that they were actually made of layers—four, five, six, or maybe eight layers of ceramics, each of which had wiring on the surface and connected to layers above and below with tiny via holes filled with metal. When the ceramics were fired, the metal wiring on the layers became hermetically sealed inside the chip carriers. The internal wiring was necessary for the inputs and outputs of the chips to do their thing.

The ceramics themselves were white porcelain-like squares made mostly of powdered aluminum oxide—the same stuff that makes up sapphire and rubies. A small amount of glass is usually added to ceramic powders so that when you fire them, they melt and fuse and sinter—the fancy name for forming strong and dense ceramics by firing them.

Normally, you fire ceramics in air, but because there were metals present, we needed to fire these particular ceramics in hydrogen to keep them from oxidizing. The metals were usually tungsten or molybdenum because these processed well at high temperatures.

The way the process worked, we would mix the ceramic and glass powders together with a binder. The binder was the same rubber used in shatterproof glass that makes up car windshields. You know how if you smash a windshield, it shatters into little tiny pieces that mostly stick together. This is because there is a thin sheet of clear rubber between two layers of glass. We used the same rubber because of its resilience and processability.

The entire mix of rubber and powders and some additives were blended with a chemical solvent- toluene. You would know the smell if you ever made plastic models as a kid. This slurry had the consistency of mayonnaise. We would pour this slurry into a hopper sitting over a moving belt covered with a sheet of clear plastic Mylar® that was a foot wide and a mile long or so. The slurry would glom onto the moving belt and there was a doctor blade a few millimeters above the plastic film that would skim a thin strip of the slurry onto the moving surface underneath. The belt would move slowly under the blade and a fairly uniform film of ceramic mayonnaise paste would cast onto the Mylar film. The toluene would begin to evaporate, and after about 60 feet, the sheet was almost completely dry, and was rolled up for storage and later use. We would call the ceramic sheet "tape" and the whole process was known as tape-casting. Tape casting is a widely practiced technology in the ceramics industry.

Later, the ceramic tape was peeled off of the Mylar®, where it was cut into smaller squares about four inches by four inches. The sheets were then patterned with small punched via holes and then silk-screened with tungsten paste that would fill the holes and form small patterns of wires on the surface. We would then take four or five of the sheets depending on the design, line up the via holes, laminate them together in a stack, and fire them in a hydrogen furnace. If everything worked out right, the final stacked sheets would form an array of chip carriers- small squares that would have a place for a chip on the surface or in a small cavity, and all the holes and wires would line up to form a nice little circuit for the chip IO's or input-output wires. Nice.

Actually, it occasionally worked. Unfortunately, this was more the exception rather than the rule. So the process that we purchased wasted a lot of time and money and materials and nobody wants that. I was called in as part of a much bigger team to solve the issue of improved yield, quality, cost, and performance of our multilayer chip carriers.

When you fire a ceramic, it shrinks when it densifies. One of the biggest issues was that each sheet did not exactly shrink the same way when fired, so that even though the holes lined up when the ceramic was "green" or unfired, by the time we got done, there were shorts and opens or worse— those nice flat sheets bowed into white potato chips or cracked and crumbled to bits.

I don't know why they exactly call unfired ceramics "green" because they are just as white going in as going out of the furnace, but that is just one of many unanswered mysteries in life that eleven seconds on Wikipedia would probably solve.

My role was to study the tape casting process. We bought and installed the Cadillac of tape casters, and instrumented the hell out of it with flow and temperature sensors. Our feeling was that, if we could understand and control the drying process, at least some of our problems would go away and our yield and performance would improve. After all, if we could just get each sheet to shrink exactly the same, then everything ought to stay aligned, flat, and stress free. Easy problem. Piece of pie, Spiro. Is tomorrow too soon to have a solution?

When we fired the ceramics, they would actually shrink a lot since the binder took up a lot of space...usually fifteen or twenty per cent. So if we started with a four-inch square, our final square might be three-and-a-half inches square when all was said and done. We used a square punch to cut out squares in the green sheet so they all started out the same. We then fired the ceramics, and used Vernier calipers to measure the shrinkage. Vernier calipers consist of a ruler with one fixed jaw at the end and one sliding jaw in the middle. When you put the fixed edge of the ceramic on one end, and slid the jaw tight on the other end of the ceramic, you could read the dimensions on the ruler and calculate your shrinkage.

Our experiments consisted of tweaking the tape casting process to see what that did to the shrinking squares that we fired in the furnace. We changed things like the height of the doctor blade, the viscosity of the ceramic slurry called the "slip" (don't ask me that one either), and the temperature of the drying zones and flow rate of the air over the drying tape and so on.

It quickly became apparent to me that the subtle changes we were making in the casting process were not getting picked up in the final fired product, at least with the clumsy Vernier calipers. In other words, the measuring tool was not sensitive enough to see the small changes that were taking place. I had the idea of making a small jig with four of the finest hypodermic needles I could find, each standing proud from the surface a millimeter so, and spaced in a perfect square. After the green sheets were cut, but before they were fired, I would imprint the surface with these needle sticks which would look like dimples or small bulls-eyes under a sensitive measuring microscope. Then when the sheet was finally fired, I would locate the dimples with a measuring microscope that was accurate to tenths of microns to see much more precisely how the sheets really shrank.

To my surprise, when I measured the squares before and after, the fired sheets were actually trapezoids! Do you remember what a trapezoid is? I suppose Webster would say a trapezoid is a quadrilateral with two parallel sides and two non-parallel sides. Picture a perfect square, and then pinch in two of the corners ever so slightly, and that is what we had.

No wonder we couldn't fire laminated stacks. They weren't perfect squares! Trapezoids shrunk more in one dimension than the other, creating misalignment and stress. OK! We are really onto something. If I could figure out what caused the trapezoids, maybe I could get rid of the issue.

So here is where the scientist goes into deep consternation, furrowed brow, pencil in hand, alone in his office, eyes shut...pencil drops and snoring commences just moments before the boss wanders in....But you know—I really did have to think long and hard over this puzzle. And finally after several days, it came to me. It really did.

I realized that while the tape was still quite wet early in the drying process, the amount of toluene left in the tape gradually became less and less as you moved along the belt. As the toluene evaporated, the rubber pulled the tiny ceramic particles closer and closer together through something called surface tension. It is kind of like the skin of Jello® pudding being tougher than the bulk. Similarly, along the edges of the drying tape, the toluene evaporated faster than in the center because it could evaporate in two dimensions—from the sides and the top, while in the center of the drying tape, if could only dry in one dimension—up. This causes the ceramic grains to dry faster on the edge than in the center and along the length, and the rubber would pull them closer together than in the center. The closer packed grains of ceramic particles in one dimension sinter and shrink less than along the other dimension and voila—you get a trapezoid instead of a square. Or so I reasoned.

This hypothesis was a breakthrough in understanding. If it was correct, then how could you fix the process? I had a rather simple solution—right at the spot where the rubber was really going from soupy wet to dry, I hung two Exacto® knives, and sliced into the surface to interrupt the surface tension in the drying slip. And when you did that, the tape stopped curling and flopped flat and when we fired it— perfect squares!

Because of this and a bunch of other improvements in the ceramics, the metal inks, the lamination process, the firing, the assembly and a countless unit operations throughout the plant, we really did make a much better product with a higher yielding process. So that when we finally gave up on this business and sold it to Coors, we probably lost less money than we would have! Put that one in your performance review and see how it flies! But at least I can go to my grave knowing that I was the one who turned trapezoids into squares. And that my story about turning trapezoids into squares is more powerful than any chemical sleep aids that you can buy with a prescription!

Lessons Learned

1. Almost every real scientific advance is associated with improved metrologies. The more you can see, the more you understand. Think about Galileo and his telescope or Leeuwenhoek with his microscope. Or in modern terms, with each new generation of powerful atom smashing accelerators, we learn more and more about time, space, atoms, subatomic particles, the creation of the universe, and why chocolate tastes so good. In this case, until I increased the measurement precision a thousand-fold, I could not even see that trapezoids were forming instead of squares, and from that, the real cause and solution to our problems were forthcoming.

2. Again, we see that there was a new observation – trapezoids- but the fundamental cause – anisotropic drying—was not immediately obvious or evident. You still 'gotta' think. Maybe someone smarter than me would have instantly known the

answer that took me days or weeks to come to—I don't know. But it sure wasn't apparent to me. And it was really nice to finally think it through, do the experiment to prove it was right, and fix the problem once and for all. Real researchers are never presented with all the data on a platter. One experiment after another uncovers new facts, and rarely do they all add up because of the random nature of data. There are always outliers and experimental errors so researchers are faced with incomplete and fuzzy data. Hypotheses are made and tested, and may or not be confirmed. Often the elegant or conclusive experiment comes after several aborted attempts to gain understanding. It is extremely frustrating for the researcher to have numerous facts that don't add up to a conclusive end. Researchers are driven to design new experiments, repeat old ones, and to gather more data—with both the expenditure of time and money that are often in short supply. For the lay businessman who may be sponsoring the project, they just don't understand why we couldn't get it right in the first place, or how it couldn't add up—how hard it is to tell the difference between a bad data point and a bad hypothesis. Sadly, the stuff in the textbooks that they studied in college had already been vetted by time and theory, making prospective science seem like fumbling around at best.

Chapter Six

All That Glitters is Not Diamond

Toward the end of my coal research, in addition to the coal-fired turbines that we saw in Chapter One, I also got involved in coal-fired diesel engines for potential use in locomotives and power generation. In a diesel, there isn't a spark like in a gasoline engine. Rather, the piston comes down the cylinder and compresses the air which makes it hot- hot enough to ignite the fuel. It's the same principal that makes your refrigerator cool but run in reverse. In our case, the fuel was coal slurry—the same kind we used in the gas turbine.

As with the turbine, there were a myriad of problems with the coal-fired diesel, most of which had workable solutions thanks to some very creative mechanical engineering and design. One ticklish problem that remained was the fuel injector. Designed to spray- atomize liquid diesel fuel, the coal slurry initially proved intractable due to plugging. With fairly extensive modifications to the fuel injector design, we were able to get the stuff to atomize and burn, but coal slurry causes severe wear on the tiny holes that the fuel goes through on way to the engine. It might work OK at first, but it doesn't take long for the fuel injector to lose its ability to atomize the slurry. Under the microscope, the perfect little round holes became fluted like the bell of a French horn. Instead of creating a fine mist, the little French horns spewed globs of coal-water-mixture. And bigger globs don't burn all the way, leading to smoke and soot.

At the time, I was carpooling to work with Bill Banholzer. Bill is an extremely talented chemical engineer with a PhD from Illinois. He since enjoyed a meteoric rise to become VP of research at GE Superabrasives, GE Lighting, GE Plastics, and in 2004, he left GE to become Chief Technology Officer for Dow Chemical, where he leads the research of the world's second largest chemical company, directing a staff in the thousands and a budget in the billions.

At the time I was working on coal-fired diesels, Bill was managing a fledgling project to make diamonds from methane gas. GE had invented Man-Made® Diamonds in 1954 using a process that copied the extreme temperatures and pressure that nature uses to make natural diamonds some three hundred miles beneath the earth's surface. In this process, carbon is mixed with special catalysts, and the mixture is then squeezed and heated in enormous presses this size of a moving van. The synthetic diamonds that form are not cubic zirconia- they are real diamonds and enjoy all the superlative properties of natural diamonds including the ability to cut and grind stone far better than anything including even natural diamonds. There is a great book entitled "The Diamond Makers" by Robert Hazen (1999) that goes through the history of this development, if you want to learn more.

In the 1960's and 1970's, a few research groups around the world including teams in Russia, Japan, and at Case Western Reserve University in Cleveland had shown that diamonds would form in low pressures when methane and hydrogen gas molecules were split using microwaves, electric arcs, or by passing the gases over a light bulb filament. One Japanese researcher even showed that if you adjusted your standard garden-variety acetylene torch just to the point where it starts to soot, you can actually get microscopic diamonds in the flame. In a few short years, making diamonds had become a high school science project! In any event, GE decided to see if there was a commercial pot of gold in low pressure diamonds and Banholzer was running the project.

As us techies do, while carpooling to CRD from nearby Glenville, we shared the problems *de jour*, in between the times we spent praising our managers and wonderful wives and the important things they do for us, of course. One day we got to talking about the wearing out of diesel engine fuel nozzles, and hatched the idea of coating them with a film of diamonds. After all, we reasoned, if diamonds are the hardest substance known to man, if anything wouldn't wear out from the shear of coal-slurry, it would be diamonds.

We worked together to develop the process and after a few clumsy attempts, we got it to work. Bill and I and a few others share a patent, "Diamond Coated Annulus..." as a result. And while the diamond coating worked OK, the coal-fired diesel joined the coal-fired turbine as yesterday's news when the price of oil plummeted in the mid eighties. Ho-hum...another successful project leads to nothing useful. This is very common in R&D, and you can't let it slow you down from inventing; as the great scientist Linus Pauling told us, the best way to have a good idea is to start with a hundred ideas.

And one very good thing came out of the joint project; at least for me. When Bill got his first major promotion, he asked me to take his job leading GE's diamond R&D; finally I would be working on something that might actually matter to the company.

The diamond business, GE Superabrasives, was under a lot of pressure (another bad pun, I know). The core business involved a very secret process to produce diamonds in enormous presses. Unfortunately, the head of GE Superabrasives R&D before Bill (how to say this delicately?) had simply stolen the technology and sold it to a Korean competitor. In case you might be worried that I am asking for a libel suit, be assured that Dr. Chien Min Sun, Ph.D from MIT, was duly tried and convicted of the charges in a US court, and spent a year in house arrest. The Wall Street Journal ran a great story about the whole mess, February 28, 1990, but in the end, despite a hard-won litigation and cease and desist order, GE had so much business with Korean interests, that we ended up not pressing the competitor who used our technology without having to pay to develop it, and they quickly tanked the synthetic diamond market.

   While at GE's central research, my group, working in a close partnership with Bill Banholzer's team in GE Superabrasives labs just outside of Columbus, Ohio, successfully developed three generations of new high-pressure diamond products that were significantly better performing and at a fraction of the cost, but in the end, the business was sold off as being too small and no longer a strategic fit with the company. It is still a successful enterprise as part of the Swedish Sandvik group today, but I will forever believe that the theft of the intellectual property was the ultimate cause of our downfall. Most industries, faced with commoditization and a ten-fold reduction in price, experience upheaval and consolidation; the superabrasives industry was no different.

   The new low-pressure diamond films business was a lot of fun because there was so much technology development in process, product, and applications. In addition to being the gemstone of choice for newlyweds, diamonds enjoy a number of superlatives that make materials scientists froth at the mouth. Besides being the hardest of all materials, diamonds also have the highest thermal conductivity along with a host of superlative mechanical, optical, acoustic, and electrical properties.

   We were able to identify and commercialize a few niche diamond film products including heat sinks for undersea telecom cables; the better heat removal, the further our customer could space the signal amplifiers, and over thousands of miles of underwater cable, the cost implications made it worthwhile.

   One interesting application was in wire-drawing dies. Wire is produced by successively pulling wire through a series of ever-so-slightly smaller holes that have been laser-drilled in a set of diamonds. This works well, but after several thousand feet of wire has been pulled through the hole in the diamond, the round hole becomes worn to an oval shape (OK—actually an ellipse for you nerds), a natural consequence of the way the carbon atoms are arranged in the diamond lattice. The upshot is that the diamonds need to be redrilled frequently and eventually need to get tossed.

I don't remember who, but someone on the team thought that diamond wire drawing dies made from the vapor process would wear out more uniformly than the natural stones. Their reasoning was that the low pressure diamonds were not made of one single crystal such as you see on a wedding ring. Rather, the diamond films are made up of clusters of thousands and thousands of tiny diamond crystals all packed together in random orientation. The idea was that, surely some of the crystals will wear a little faster than others, but on average, the hole should stay round since other microcrystals would have a different orientation that was more wear- resistant.

We made up some test wire drawing dies from the vapor diamonds, and they worked as predicted- the holes and wires indeed stayed perfectly round. Project done? Ring the cash register? Not so fast! This is real life we are talking about. This is yet another battle in the R&D war- solve one problem and create two more! Let's hear it for job-security.

It seems that those oh-so-small spaces between the tiny crystals were just enough to cause scratches on the metal wire, and our customer wanted smooth wires.

Materials scientists call these spaces between the microcrystals "grain boundaries." Whenever microscopic crystals abut, the atoms between the crystals are ever-so-slightly weaker than the ones in the middle of the crystal simply because the atoms in the bulk are perfectly bonded to maximize the strength of the crystal, while the ones in the gap are off kilter. As a result, they wear faster, leaving a surface imperfection that gets transferred to the wire. In other words- scratches. Back to the drawing board.

In one of those massive three-way videoconferences, we had a brainstorming session. Always being the first to suggest dumb ideas, I asked the experts, "What if we made up the wire dies, and then annealed them by putting them into the press that we used for growing high pressure diamonds? Wouldn't that get rid of the grain boundaries?" Expecting the usual seventeen reasons why that was a dumb idea, in fact, Tom Anthony- the most brilliant GE inventor since Thomas Edison- sat up in his chair and said,

"That might work." And it did! We packed some of those suckers in the pressure chamber and cooked them to twenty-five thousand atmospheres pressure and four thousand degrees F, and *voila*- the cracks were mostly gone. Wow.

As it turns out—"mostly gone" and "all gone" were not quite the same thing, at least the customer felt, and so "mostly gone" was good enough for another patent, but "all gone" was needed to make a sale. Darn those customers! No sale again. Rats.

Ahh, but always thinking, it now occurred to me that if we could fix the flaws in a synthetic wire die, maybe we could fix the flaws in a natural diamond. Here's real money! After all, a flawed one-carat gemstone might sell for a hundred bucks, but a perfect stone would sell for ten thousand.

So I went out and got some really awful natural diamonds, little triangular things called macles that were filled with cracks and black specks, and my fabulous associate, Herb Peters, cooked them up. But each time I looked at them before and after- well they just didn't improve very much. After a month or two of trying, I gave up.

I moved on from leading GE's diamond R&D to our rubber business shortly after that (see Chapters Seven through Thirteen), but my good pal Tom Anthony is much smarter and more tenacious than I am, and after I was long-gone, he continued to poke at the idea of improving natural diamonds. Eventually he and Steve Webb and others figured out the trick.

For one thing, I should not have started out with such awful diamonds where a change would be hard to see; I should have started with diamonds that were close to perfect, but with a special kind of flaw that is amenable to improvement. They figured out which diamonds would benefit from a little nudge, you know twenty-five kilobars, four-thousand degrees F…and they got the process to work. They were able to buy these diamonds dirt cheap on the open market, and created a successful and thriving new product called Bellataire® using natural diamonds that are truly forever (or at least a billion years old or so) but which experienced a few growing pains on the way up to the surface of the earth, and just needed a little adjustment like a chiropractor might do to your back. The Bellataire® stones are beautiful and they sell at a fraction of the cost of a purely natural diamond, so what started as a wire-die project, eventually found its way to the marketplace. Score one for the good guys!

And for those of you who might be thinking, "Why tell anyone they have been treated and sell them for a discount?" Honestly it would be nigh impossible for a customer or even an expert to know if the stones had been altered, but GE is really a company of integrity and it would have been unthinkable to do otherwise. Surely a company as large as GE had a few bad apples, and every few years someone would bend the rules, get caught, and make headlines. After all, people are people. But as a rule, we ran the company on the up and up.

Lessons Learned

1.   If you are going to try to solve a problem, start at the easiest place, not the hardest. By using the most-flawed diamonds, I thought I would see the starkest improvement, but in fact, any changes were obscured. Only by starting with near-perfect diamonds were we able to achieve perfection, and perfection is where the big money is.

2.   Diamonds may be the superlative in materials science, but that alone does not guarantee a large and profitable market. For one thing, many of the desirable properties of diamonds are overwhelmed by the flaws that occur at grain boundaries, as we saw with wire dies. Even when near-perfect diamond films were successfully produced, the huge market did not materialize as production costs were high and we were limited in the size and shape of the product. Also, the diamond films generally needed to be bonded to another surface,

often using a process known as brazing which is an ultra-soldering like process. As you might guess, the braze became the weakest link in the eventual product, and sacrificed much of the diamond's performance.

3. Loss of IP, either naturally or illicitly, can commoditize a market, and eventually will cause dramatic losses in profitability, industry upheaval and commoditization. Assuming that this is inevitable, the winning strategy is to continue to out-innovate your competition and stay ahead.

4. Combining people and projects and ideas- in this case, diamond films and fuel nozzles- is the surest way to innovation. Innovation does not occur in a vacuum.

5. As the boss, I always liked to be the first to propose dumb ideas in order to make others comfortable to do the same. In many R&D cultures, people just clam up because they don't want to appear dumb, and a lot of good stuff gets left behind. Often someone smart- in this case Tom Anthony and Steve Webb—can take a basically dumb idea (Spiro) and turn it into a good one. Plus it is important to find and grow people who will tell the boss he is full of crap—that science is their turf, not mine. And every now and then, I might just have an idea worth pursuing, and that really scares the troops.

Chapter Seven

Rubber Man

My next job was leading GE's silicone rubber research and development team. My personal transition from diamonds to rubber is a vignette worth hearing, because changing fields in science and technology is relatively unusual given the premium value placed on deep expertise.

As I mentioned in the last chapter, diamond films can be made by decomposing methane gas and hydrogen, simply passing them through an arc, a microwave, or even through a tungsten light bulb filament. If a nearby surface is made up of the right material and at the right temperature, microscopic diamond crystals will form, and eventually cover the entire surface. My group was working on all aspects of process and product development of these diamond films.

As a side "bootleg" project (one that was not officially approved), I had the idea of using fluorinated methane instead of pure methane. Methane has the formula CH_4, in which there are four hydrogen atoms for each carbon atom. A fluorinated methane might have the formula CH_3F or CH_2F_2, in which one or more of the hydrogen atoms is substituted with a fluorine atom. I thought that if I could get some fluorine incorporated into the diamond lattice, it would form a tough, non-stick composition, kind of like a cross between diamond and Teflon® which is the famous DuPont polymer made up of fluorinated hydrocarbons. And indeed, the product of diamond growth with fluorocarbons did exactly that.

Once again, finding an application for the product was my new challenge. As most researchers learn the hard way, technology pushes rarely work. A technology push is where you invent something and look for a use, whereas a technology pull is when the market has a need that you try to fulfill through discovery. Market pulls usually work since someone told you they would buy it if you could just get it to do such and such. Then when you deliver, they at least feel guilty when they tell you to pound salt. Actually, they don't feel guilty at all. I think they enjoy it, kind of like Lucy pulling the football out from Charlie Brown. But at least, for a while we could labor under some hope that there would a customer at the end of the dark, dark tunnel.

One area of possible interest in hard diamond fluoride films was in anti-ice coatings for jet engines. Occasionally, ice will build up on the spinner—that little circle in the center of a jet engine that you might see if you are sitting in a window seat in front of a plane and look backwards at the engines. A whole bunch of important engineers and managers from GE Aircraft Engines, located just outside on Cincinnati, met with me to talk about coatings and materials to fix the problem. We thought that the diamond-like carbon fluoride might be so slippery and tough that the ice would come right off.

It didn't. Almost end of story.

A few months later, this same group of GE Aircraft engineering brass got involved in what they called "laminar flow nacelle." The nacelle (pronounced 'nuh-sell') is the shell that houses the jet engines. Some folks at NASA figured out that if we could manufacture a perfectly smooth nacelle, then airflow over the surface would follow the streamlines and would have very low friction and resistance. But if the surface was rough and bumpy, there would be turbulence, and it would slow the plane down a little bit. How rough? Would you believe a speck, maybe a tenth the diameter of a human hair, would be big enough to destroy the laminar flow. It might not seem like a big deal, but if we could pull off laminar flow, the savings in fuel would be staggering— the kind of efficiency gains that normally take several generations of materials and design improvements. And with modern manufacturing and materials, it was now possible to produce a perfect nacelle.

But there was just one problem....bug splatters!

Every time the plane would take off or land, some bugs would splatter onto the nacelle surface and stick like crazy, undoing all the hard work of the designers and manufacturers. What's an aircraft engine manufacturer going to do?

Fortunately, the folks from GE Aircraft remembered me and my diamond-fluoride failures and asked me to join their effort to keep bugs from sticking to airplanes, and to not limit the possible solutions to just diamond-fluoride. The entire materials world was my oyster.

I decided to give it a try for several reasons. I thought it was a good, interesting problem; I wanted to serve my company and customer; and mostly, I was being measured by how many research dollars I brought into the laboratory (remember Chapter Four?), and every little bit helped. You don't turn down paying customers.

I joined forces with a combustion engineer named Tom Fric. Tom had constructed a massive wind tunnel, and our plan was to take insects and splatter them onto various surfaces at three hundred miles per hour, and see what stuck. Or what didn't.

We actually ordered a bunch of insect larvae- for flies and moths, mosquitoes and beetles—then hatched them, and sucked them into the wind tunnel. Our project had a huge curiosity factor given the nursery we built. Tom also put together a high speed vision system that took thousands of frames per second and allowed us to observe in super-slow-motion, the splatters. People just loved watching movies of bugs spattering in ultra-slow-motion!

Meanwhile, drama notwithstanding, my job was to come up with a bunch of materials to test. What a hoot! Just think—eight years of formal education put to use swatting flies! My mother would be proud.

Yes we tried diamond-like carbon fluoride, along with a bunch of metal, ceramic, and plastic coatings, and nothing worked particularly well. Until we tried a very special form of silicone rubber that GE had developed for the purpose of preventing zebra mussels and barnacles from attaching to boats. This rubber was pretty tough, but also included special oil that was trapped in between the rubber molecules. The oil would oh-so-slowly weep to the surface of the rubber, keeping it continuously moist, wet, and slippery. Indeed, neither zebra mussel nor barnacle could get a toehold on the slime, and the stuff worked beautifully for its intended purpose. It also worked great for bug splatters. The rubber was resilient, and as we observed in our movies, most of the bugs bounced of the surface without even rupturing. For the very few that did splatter, the bug guts beaded up and quickly rolled off the surface.

The real proof is in the pudding, as the expression goes, so we went to NASA's John Glenn facility in Cleveland, coated up the tip tanks on a NASA Learjet, and took off, flying up and down the cornfields of Ohio at low altitude, leaving countless insect remains in our wake. After a few hours, we stopped the plane, got out, looked at the coated (and uncoated) tip tanks and by golly the coating was clean as a whistle…it really worked!

The customer was thrilled (until their funding got cut and the project was cancelled, but by now you should have expected this) and I got another useless couple patents "Insect Abatement System." Almost end of project.

Having a solution looking for a problem, getting rid of bug splatters, we thought about who else might be interested, and contacted car makers including NASCAR. The NASCAR guys were really interested not because their cars would go faster, but because their logos might stay clean of tire dust, and be as bright and readable at the end of the race as they were at the start. Let's not kid ourselves, NASCAR is all about the logos. My administrative assistant shamelessly squealed like a stuck- pig every time Kyle Petty's team called me on the phone, and when we got some race car parts to coat, she would rub them all over her body when they arrived in the mail before handing them to me. Hmmm I wonder if her cheap perfume had something to do with them not working. Because unfortunately, the tire dust never stuck better than with our coatings.

By now, I hope you are seeing a pattern of problems being tossed my way, followed by a lucky, heroic, elegant, or clumsy solution, none of which finds its way to the light of day for a variety of technical, commercial or political reasons. You really want to understand R&D? One of my professors, Lenny Stephenson at Stanford, said that [for a career in research and development] "You need to have a well- developed sense of delayed gratification." Delayed? How about never?

It is the great lie that the technologists are the main reason that advances don't succeed. Sure we are part of the problem and part of the solution, but the world is much, much bigger than we are. R&D is a very easy, convenient target to scapegoat, somewhat akin to blaming the guy who struck out with two outs in the ninth. But more often than not, we are assigned the wrong problem, and when we eventually solve it, nobody cares. Or we find two new problems that make the original solution no good. At least— we never run out of problems to work on, and maybe someday something will click.

My first foray into silicones turned out to not be a total waste of time. About the time I was finishing up the bug splatter project, a job came open to lead the silicone rubber engineering group and I was invited to interview for it. I imagine their thinking was, "Here's a guy who splatters bugs for a living—working for GE Silicones in Waterford, NY might actually be an improvement."

The boss eventually told me I wasn't the right guy for the job, but that he was going to have some other openings soon, and I should apply for them. Sure enough, the silicone sealants team was looking for a new leader and I was brought in. Sealants are those tubes you see at Home Depot and Lowes with the plastic tip that you snip off, plop into your caulking gun, and squeeze away until you get a nice bead of rubber. The rubber flows easily at first, but after a couple hours, it cures and forms a nice seal for windows, tubs and showers, etc.

I spent a great day interviewing with the very talented and capable sealants research team and their business and manufacturing partners. At the end of the day, Wayne Delker, the head of R&D and now CTO at Clorox, brought me into his office and said that I did great in the interviews, and that he had only one question: "If you had a choice between leading a high-performing team of talented scientists and engineers, or leading a dysfunctional group of misfits, which would you choose?" In a nanosecond I said, "Give me the misfits any day!" Wayne said, "Great—you have the job... but leading the Rubber group, not the Sealants group." And so it came to be.

Lessons Learned

1. Again we see that what I legitimately worked on – diamond fluoride as a new, high-performance material- went nowhere. Actually, I recently heard from an old friend Karen Gleason, an MIT professor, that she and a spinoff company of hers were looking at the stuff. So I hope it flies somewhere. But the material got me introduced to anti-icing coatings for jet engines which also went nowhere, and that led to insect coatings for jet engines. The diamond fluoride still didn't work, but silicones used for zebra mussels did work. Such is the tortuous path of R&D. And once again, even though the project worked technically, there was no dough at the end of the tunnel for a variety of commercial and political reasons. But it did lead to a new job for me where I could continue my stellar career of making useless inventions and accumulating value-less patents, occasionally interrupted briefly with a commercial success that blazed in glory for an hour or two before the next problem would surface.

2. Growing bugs from larvae is pretty cool, especially when you are getting paid. Splattering them at three hundred miles an hour and looking at the splatters at ten thousand frames a second is also cool. Flying around in a Learjet at fifty feet above

the cornfields of Ohio is also cool. Being a scientist has its rewards—not usually financial but there can be lots of fun and great stories. Don't underestimate the "cool" factor in choosing a life.

3.   Once again we see that solving the technical problem is no guarantee of commercial success.

Chapter Eight
The Rubber Factory

I love factories. Even rubber factories. When I was in college, one summer I worked in a rubber factory where we made car mats. It was hot and stinky and every day I would come home looking like a raccoon with white eyes where my goggles were, and black everywhere else. It was a blast.

At GE, over the years I got to walk through and study many of our factories including ones that make jet engines, locomotives, plastics, ceramics, motors, and CT scanners. I have a real soft spot for factories and the people who make them work making things for the rest of us. So when I first landed at GE Silicones, I was delighted that the labs were right next to the plant.

My first month on the job, I decided to spend each day working in the labs, then throw on coveralls and a hard hat, and go out onto the plant floor to watch and help them make rubber. Since this was a union factory, I couldn't really help by like touching anything, but I could sit in the control room and watch the operators do what they did, learning to mumble at the right times and even learned to groan the proper way when something bad happened. I didn't ask for permission from anyone because forgiveness is always easier to get than permission. I just told the operators that I was new and from R&D and just wanted to learn about how we made rubber. They didn't need to know that I was the section manager of the rubber group...I was just people. They treated me well, glad that I took an interest in them personally and their work and process. I learned a lot. Later when I would need favors from them, this really came in handy, but I would be lying if I said that I anticipated that.

One night at around eleven PM, coming off the shift in my dirty, sweaty coveralls, I was making it back to my office in the R&D building when Dave Cote, our CEO wandered by. Dave looked at me, squinted, finally recognized me and asked me what I was doing. I explained that I was spending my first month working the second shift in Production just to learn how rubber really was made. He smiled and thought that was a terrific idea. Dave was known as a really tough SOB, a reputation he would carry to GE Appliances as their next CEO, then to TRW as CEO, and finally ten-plus wildly successful years as Honeywell CEO. I think after that, he cut me some slack and treated me more kindly. Like the time several months later (Chapter Twelve), when he and I were screaming and spitting at each other in the parking lot, kicking dirt on each other's shoes like a blind umpire and crusty old manager going at it after a bad call (Dave's)...I think he only kicked dirt on my shoes instead kicking in my shins because of those lingering kind thoughts from my first nights on the plant floor.

From those first early days, I always made sure I attended the seven AM Production meeting with all of the plant managers. Here they would go over the problem's *de jour*—missing raw materials, quality failures, back orders, and especially to blame R&D for inventing crappy products that they couldn't produce. I was always there to listen to the issues, defend my group when called for, take blame when appropriate, and to really help solve the problems. I was usually the only R&D guy there, and it was just part of the regular cadence of my day. And at least when my boss would come after me about a problem, I had already heard about it and was taking action.

Like I said—I have a warm spot for manufacturing.

Around this time, GE was getting engaged in six sigma—the systematic process for improving everything from new products, manufacturing, shipping, billing...even hiring.

My first six sigma project was all about getting R&D projects done faster, because as everyone by now knows, R&D projects are always too slow, cost too much, and never deliver to expectations.

One of the nice things about having research and production co-located is that you can run experimental products on the actual equipment used in production. This should save a step and save time in principle. But in practice, Manufacturing wants to produce products they can sell, and they are measured on how much they produce. So R&D is basically a disruption to them. It would take a lot of pressure by the business general manager to get Operations to squeeze in an experiment or new product.

For my first six-sigma project, I discovered that, at the end of each quarter, and especially at the end of the fiscal year, Operations wouldn't interrupt production for anything or anybody. In fact, they only made the fastest, easiest high-volume grades because once the product passed inspection, it became "Finished Goods" and was valued on the books, helping us "make the quarter." Usually, "making the quarter" began two weeks before the end of the quarter, and "making the year" began four-to-six weeks before the end of the year. So progress in R&D was basically halted, along with customer sampling for two-plus-two-plus-two-plus-six weeks each year.

I was able to show that the new products carried a much higher profit margin, and that by systematically delaying them an accumulated twelve weeks a year by this practice, we were costing the company a lot of money. As a result, through my six sigma logic, along with begging and bribery, at least the rubber team was able to get experiments done even during crunch time. Woohoo! I know that this is logically the right thing to do, but I am certain that if I wasn't always present on the production floor and at morning production meetings, I would have had no friends out there to buy into these plans. Science, technology, production, suppliers, quality—they are all people first and foremost and need lots of TLC- tender loving care.

Lessons Learned

1.   Manufacturing is a really good place to learn how science and technology really get practiced. It is important to understand how the production folks are measured, and help them be successful by helping with quality and yield issues and not designing un- manufacturable difficult products.

2.   Accidentally getting on your CEO's good side is also nice, even if their memories are short. I didn't tell anyone about my stint in Operations because I didn't want to get turned away, but I was kind of glad someone noticed, especially the toughest boss in the company.

3.   The whole scheduling and queuing process in Operations is one critical step in accelerating, or decelerating the introduction of new products. If your Operations folks aren't cut some slack for interrupting their process to introduce new things, it can be a disaster. That's why partnering with your Operations leader is one key in speed-to-market of new stuff.

Chapter Nine

Silicone Rubber Keypads, Part One

When you type on your keyboard, the keys all press down and spring back with a high degree of uniformity, at least until one of them sticks. Don't you just hate that? There actually aren't any springs in your keyboard— just a small dome sheet of silicone rubber. When you press down on the dome, it makes an electrical connection underneath, and then it springs back.

At GE Silicones, we made a special grade of rubber that our customer, Keytronic, used to mold the dome sheets. At the time, 1995, keyboards and computers were designed to last a lot longer than they do nowadays, and we were charged with making the rubber work the same, year in and year out, for thirty million cycles. We even had a special machine that would tap away for those millions of cycles. We used to pay people to do the testing, but the work was too stimulating for them and they decided to become accountants, instead; so we had to invent a keypad testing machine. Our stuff really worked great.

The dome sheet is rather complicated. There are over a hundred keys on a keyboard when you include all the letters, numbers, punctuation, and those F keys and special keys that only the nerds know how to use. Our customer used a mold with those hundred+ domes plus all the space in between plus runners to flow the rubber. In order to mold the dome sheet, one of our brilliant chemists, Ed Jeram, invented a special rubber called

LIM® which stands for Liquid Injection Molded silicone. It comes in two parts just like an epoxy, and it has the viscosity of Vaseline® — barely thin enough to pump and fill the entire mold, and cure, all in around twenty seconds. It worked well, but it wasn't cheap.

Coming into 1995, keyboards cost around a hundred dollars. By the end of 1996, they were down to thirteen dollars and would be below seven dollars soon enough. Our customer was really struggling as you can imagine, and feared that they would lose their business to low-cost Chinese products. In fact, they were nearing desperation, as was our own sales team who was afraid of losing a big chunk of business. They were all so desperate, that they even brought me out to Spokane to join the VP's and Sales Managers in a pow-wow with the customer to see if we could find a way to save the business.

When I walked into the plant, I was struck with how many drums of product they were using every day. In fact, we were barely able to keep up with their needs though our mixer was running to capacity. I was also aware that we used a very special, dangerous, and expensive process to treat one of our raw materials not once, but twice, in order to give the product a one year shelf life. I was also aware that we were running out of treating capacity and were about to invest several million dollars to make a new treater. So I said to the customer, "If you can live with a shorter shelf life product—say six weeks instead of a year—I might be able to get you a much cheaper product." It was like throwing a lifebuoy to a drowning man. They went for it and it worked just fine, keeping them in business for another three years or so-until succumbing to the inevitable.

The regional sales manager was so pleased, he asked what I might want for recognition. I told him I always wanted to go to a San Francisco to watch the 49ers, so one Saturday, I flew out to San Fran in time for a quick tailgate party, then into Candlestick to see Jerry Rice and Joe Montana, then home just like that! Score one for the good guys.

Lessons Learned

1. Sometimes, we design in features (long shelf life) that don't matter to customers, but which they end up unknowingly paying for to nobody's satisfaction. Make sure you really understand their needs. If you can delight them with more than they need and no additional cost—great! If not, don't overdesign a product just because you can or think you need to.

2. Always bring your R&D guy to meet with the customers. Sure we know too much and are too honest and are a bit nerdy, but to your customer, we can be endearing and add to your credibility. Moreover, we actually know useful stuff that you really have no business knowing. In this example, I knew that we gave the product a one-year shelf life, and that we had an expensive process and ingredient that was running low on capacity that was required to extend the shelf life- all of which could be sacrificed. That's way out of scope for any salesman.

3. Creating free capacity is a great way to save your company money and free up cash. Before you build any new unit operations, check to see if you can shortcut the process, make a substitution, or design around otherwise. Several years later while at Nalco, we were running out of capacity for a process to make colloidal silica- small spheres of microscopic sand that are used to reinforce paper. When I reviewed the manufacturing process, I found that the stuff cooked for exactly one shift. Hmmm. Now if I see a process that runs for 6.2 hours or 11.3 hours, I will believe that it has been optimized. Anything that runs for eight, twelve, twenty-four hours, or basically any even number was probably designed for the convenience of the workforce, and can be improved.

Chapter Ten

Silicone Rubber Keypads, Part Two

In the last chapter, I wrote about the best, high-end computer keypads designed to last thirty million cycles. At the low end of the spectrum are silicone rubber keypads used in calculators and car keys, for example-- items that only need to last tens of thousands of cycles. Here—the main thing that matters is price. There is a big market for cheap keypads and the rubber that goes into them.

Before we get to the meat-and-potatoes of this twisted tale, please bear with me for a moment as I describe the three major decisions we have to make in the manufacture of rubber. You don't need to pay too much attention to the details- just gloss through this. Just remember that there are three choices we basically need to make.

First—we can mix the stuff up cold in something called a Banbury Mixer or we can cook the stuff hot in something called a dough mixer. A Banbury mixer takes a couple minutes to mix all the components, while a doughmixer takes twelve hours or so and uses a lot of energy;. I bet you know which process is a lot cheaper and I also bet you also know that the quality of cooked rubber is much better than that cold-mixed stuff.

Second- we can use fumed silica to add to the silicone gums for strength, or we can add precipitated silica. Fumed silica is costly, and is produced by burning silanes, forming a fluffy snow-white powder that makes a very strong, but costly rubber. Precipitated silica is made by a wet process from sand, and is dirt cheap but as you might guess, also gives an inferior rubber. Does anything cheaper and easier ever produce a superior product?

Third, we can cure the rubber with peroxides or we can use a platinum catalyst. As you might guess—peroxides are cheap and give an inferior product and platinum is expensive but gives a superior product.

So you see- we have three choices- Banbury cold or doughmixer hot; precipitated silica or fumed silica; and peroxide or platinum cure. In each case, the latter costs more and gives a better product.

While touring huge cities in China that you probably never heard of – Bao Ding, Zibo, Jinan, Nantong, Nanjing in search of rubber business opportunities —I got to thinking about how to make a cheaper better rubber and came up with this truth table:

	A	B	C	D	E	F	G	H
Banbury	A	B	C	D				
Doughmixer					E	F	G	H
Platinum	A		C		E		G	
Peroxide		B		D		F		H
Fumed Silica	A	B			E	F		
Precipitated Silica			C	D			G	H

The truth table above shows all the possible ways to make rubber given the three major choices. For example, Rubber A uses a Banbury cold mixer, platinum cure, and fumed silica. Rubber B uses a Banbury cold mixer, peroxide cure and fumed silica. As you can see from the table, given two choices of three variables (silica type, cure chemistry, mixing process), we end up with eight possibilities- what the statisticians call "permutations". I'm not sure anyone ever looked at the rubber world this way. But when I did, it opened all sorts of possibilities. The cheapest of all worlds was Banbury cold mix with peroxide cure and precipitated silica. I was told that we tried it and the rubber was weaker than cheese. Oh well; if only mice were buying.

The others were all successful commercial grades, especially the cold mix Banbury grades which were cheap, great, and sold by the ton as Silplus®. The other grades we made lots of were doughmixer, platinum cure, fumed silica which went by the Tufel® trade name and gave very high performance, and the doughmixer, precipitated silica, peroxide cure that we made in our Japan partnership with Toshiba Silicones.

Still awake?

Salient by its absence was the grade made with platinum cure, Banbury cold mixer, and precipitated silica. We call these gaps generically "White Space," because the page for this grade consists of a blank white sheet of paper.

Curious about this gap, I asked one of my outstanding chemists, Yi Feng Wang, to estimate the cost of a grade like this, and remarkably, it was really cheap. Yi Feng went to the lab, made up a bunch of this stuff, tested it, and found that it was also remarkably strong. We knew that cheap and strong ought to be perfect for low grade keypads, and by golly it was!

Time to print money and have Spiro and Wang ride off into the sunset as a famous R&D heroes! Move over Bill Gates and Steve Jobs.

Oh yes....but...oops. Small problem. Did you expect this by now? Good— you are learning about the real life of R&D.

There is always a "But," don't you think? Commercializing R&D is never easy. But this 'but' was a different 'but' than the usual 'buts'. Most buts include patents and IP, market, cost, manufacture, distribution, permit, performance, toxicity....we had none of the above.

It turns out that our Banbury mixers were located in Waterford, New York, and our customers were in China and served by our Ohta, Japan factory and Japanese sales team. Of course, if we made the rubber in the US and shipped it to China, this would work out beautifully for our customer and the company. They would get cheap, high-performing rubber which is what they wanted, and we would make lots of money. Outstanding. But it would also have required taking work away from our Japanese factory that was using doughmixers and who had no Banbury mixers. The Japanese sales team did not want to take work and jobs away from their factory, especially one which was only half-owned by the Japanese company and half-owned by GE. In Japan, there are more important considerations than company profitability and sales, especially the care and feeding of their employees-for-life. Also, since the Banbury mixers were located in NY, the American business manager didn't want to use them to produce rubber intended for China, because the Japanese sales team would get the sales credit toward their bonus, and at the same time, the American team would actually lose sales and their bonus would shrink because the mixers wouldn't be available for working on US products and US sales. So despite the fact that we had the best and cheapest product for the customer, neither the Japanese nor American business teams were incented to give it to them and the project died on the vine. *C'est le vie*. Score another losing project for Spiro and the R&D team. Wow this guy really knows how to waste money!

Lessons Learned.

1. Looking for White Space in the design or market is a great way to systematically uncover untested opportunities. Try to think of all combinations and permutations of features and benefits and ingredients and processes, and see if any are missing. If you find some, fill the void and see if anyone is interested. And don't be shy about going beyond cheap/expensive and low/high performance. There are often hidden features that will surprise you.

2. In general, cheap means lower quality. Nature is a cruel mistress indeed. But very rarely, she will smile upon you. Look for these moments and find ways to exploit them. Aluminum is a great example.

Early in the commercial development of aluminum, it was fantastically lightweight, conductive and strong. But horrifically expensive. Then the Bayer process came along, and we got our cake and ate it, too. Aluminum is a huge part of our economy as a result.

3. It is nice to focus on customer needs, product design and benefits, and by putting the two together, you find a winner. But you also need to think about people and organizations. In this case, we had a good niche product, but we failed to meet the requirements of the Japan team (full employment in the factory) or the American team (big bonuses) and the project failed. Often, there are many people along the road to perdition....oops I meant road to commercialization... who have agendas. Lawyers want to avoid liability and patent fights; Manufacturing wants to avoid investment and cost; Quality wants to avoid scrap and testing; Sales wants to avoid cannibalization; Regions want to avoid transfer costs; Logistics wants to avoid bottlenecks and transportation costs; Finance wants to avoid everything that costs money or has risk. Do you see a theme? R&D is continuously pushing a rope through a huge gauntlet made up of everyone from customers, competitors, regulators, and especially the people on their own team. And then we get hammered when it falls through or takes too long. I'm sure the Finance guys or lawyers have their own fine whine, but hey—write your own damn book! This is my soapbox.

Chapter Eleven

When Left is Right and Right Is Wrong

In any real process, from day to day or batch to batch, things are never exactly the same. The raw materials have some degree of variation, and the processes and tests also fluctuate, sometimes in a normal statistical way, and sometimes they drift for reasons that are systematic, accidental, inadvertent, or deliberate. Pipes and valves and pumps wear out, surfaces corrode, weights and measures drift, and sometimes the stuff you think you added is off just a bit in quality or quantity. Often these changes don't matter, and then all of a sudden, they do.

We used to say, in the Silicone business, that "A Little Piece of Waterford (our NY plant) goes out in every product;" in this case, in the form of black specks from the corrosion of the aging facility. Sometimes the specks got so bad, especially in our clearest medical grade tubing, that our customers would reject a batch.

There is so much variation that products will naturally drive in and out of specification. A customer may be using one of our products for a particular application, and it will have been working fine for months at a time, and then all of a sudden, wham- it no longer works. They get very upset about this and want to know what we changed. Maybe nothing! Now what?

In all my businesses, we had carefully prescribed "change control" procedures. We basically could not change anything without going over the changes in a formal review.

Some changes required customer approval, others just required that we inform customers, and some were so minor that we just went ahead and did them. A big one would include changing a raw material supplier from one vendor to the next, in which case, a number of trials needed to be performed to show that there was no difference. You'd be amazed at how changing the supplier of a simple, pure compound such as HCl or methanol would still cause us major headaches, simply because these were 99.5% pure, and it was the other 0.5% that could ruin your life for several weeks.

But as I alluded to earlier, it wasn't the changes you made that caused you problems, it was when you didn't make changes and the product still flew out of control—this really caused headaches.

And even if the product returned to normal after a week or two, if you didn't know what happened and why, it made us and our customers very nervous to continue with us as a now-unreliable supplier. And this happened all the time. It was rare that some excursion wasn't happening somewhere, if not several at the same time. So R&D was frequently deeply involved in collecting retained samples of finished goods and raw materials, reviewing process control charts, and going back to our vendors to do the same. As you might imagine, vendors aren't exactly welcoming when you want to go in to find out exactly what they were doing and what changes they made, since whatever they were supplying us was highly proprietary to them, along with their costs. Plus— what if they really screwed up? They might have to pay retribution or worse—get sued or fired. So things got really messy during excursions, and often we felt like we weren't getting the whole story from our suppliers; and sadly, our customers often felt that way about us.

A phenomenal amount of effort from my teams, in all of my jobs, was firefighting—chasing down why good products suddenly were failing, and trying to mollify angry customers. It was always a challenging "CSI" Crime Scene Investigator detective effort to find "the smoking gun"—the thing that really changed and caused the product to fail. The real issue wasn't finding the one thing that changed- in reality it was that everything was constantly changing, and perhaps nobody did anything deliberate to change the process at all—it just drifted out of whack. But which part was causing us the issue?

Consider fumed silica—an important ingredient in rubber, as well as in the polishing compounds we will discuss in later chapters. Fumed silica is made by burning silanes—small molecules usually containing one silicon atom and four chlorine atoms in the case of silicon tetrachloride. When put into a flame, the byproducts would be HCl (hydrogen chloride) and fumed silica. Fumed silica was white as snow, and the structure was even something like a snowflake when looked at under high magnification. The experts call the structure "fractal," and I bet if you looked up "fractal" on Google or Wikipedia, you would see some pretty pictures of things with unusual repeat geometry.

You know how no two snowflakes are identical; it is the same with fumed silica. Try and run a repeatable process using that stuff!

When the silanes go through the flame, it is so hot that all the atoms fly apart, and then when the gases move past the flame, they rapidly cool and condense into the snow-like powder. Very fascinating stuff. Sometimes, the stuff would stick to the walls, or instead of flying out of the burner, might fly back in a recirculation pattern and melt into ice-balls instead of snow. As you can imagine, ice balls and recirculated or caked on silica behaved very differently from the good fumed silica powder.

And sometimes, other impurities from upstream would cake on the walls, and maybe break off every now and then and accidentally become part of the fumed silica. Or even if it didn't spall off, it would add just enough insulation to change the cooling and quenching cycle ever so slightly, but enough to change some minor property of the fumed silica, and the resulting rubber was too stiff or too weak. Who knew?

Even the ultrapure tetrachlorosilane would occasionally become contaminated with a trace amount of another tramp material, and it would get incorporated into the fumed silica. Sometimes these tramp materials didn't matter and sometimes they did. I remember that a very small amount of boron would wreak havoc with the structure of the fumed silica, for example, as borosilicates are very sticky.

And fumed silica is just one of a dozen or so components in rubber or our polishing compounds or paper additives, any one of which can go wrong and mess up a batch. And you don't know which—just that the rubber isn't as strong or resilient as it was last week. Now go figure out what went wrong and how to fix it. And make sure it never happens again.

So instead of doing research, everyone drops everything to figure out where the culprit was, and how to fix it. And more often than not, at first blush nothing changed! Yipes!

I will tell you that in one case, at an unnamed business with an unnamed customer, we really did deliberately change something and not tell them. It was one of the darkest moments in my career, and makes for an interesting and relevant vignette.

To begin with, did you know that certain molecules are left and right handed? The two types of molecules are basically the same, just like your left and right hand are basically the same, but they are also somewhat different. We call them "enantiomers" and we literally describe them as L for left handed, and D for right handed, named after the way levelose and dextrose sugars polarize light. For example, in the sleep aid, Lunesta ®, the active ingredient is the left handed version and it will put you to sleep if you swallow it. The right-handed version will only put you to sleep by reading about it. Otherwise it is physiologically inactive.

One of our products used the L version of a raw material and for years, it worked fine for our customers. Often, pure L or pure D versions of a molecule cost more than a mixture of the two. Somebody in our raw-materials-sourcing operation was going through catalogues from suppliers, and saw a very inexpensive version of the chemical we were using which happened to be a blend of the L and D; he reasoned that it would save us lots of money by making the switch. The folks in production made up a batch and it passed all the tests, and they decided to make the change. And they also didn't want to tell the customer, because they didn't want to share the savings with them. Normally if you make a swap that saves you money, the customers also want a share of the savings, so our business team decided not to tell them. Bad decision.

A lot of small changes like this take place every day in every industry, and you can't really be troubled by small changes, the vast majority of which go unnoticed by anyone. Until it bites you, and like the woman who backed into the fan... "Disaster!" Like this time.

After so many years of perfect quality and performance, our customer was naturally peeved and perplexed and wanted to know what changed.

And we lied.

With a straight-ish face, the business manager, the R&D manager, the quality manager, and the production manager all said the same thing, that something in our raw material stream had changed, that our supplier fixed it and it will never happen again; indeed all the batches returned to normal after that.

And the customer didn't buy it for one second. Maybe they were just too smart, or maybe one our guys wasn't a very good liar. But as a result, we lost a lot of their business and their trust forever.

I personally wanted us to go back to the customer and own up to our guilt, beg forgiveness, and promise it would never happen again, but I was overruled. What do R&D guys know, anyway? Oh well.

I assure you that this was the only time in thirty years that I ever heard of my company lying to a customer, but years later it tastes just as bad as it did then.

And of course, this stuff probably happened to us all the time from our suppliers. And worse was when we did it to ourselves.

Occasionally, one of our products would fail and R&D would get blamed for the failure because we had obviously designed a crappy product that nobody could make, and then we were charged with fixing it. After several weeks of CSI investigation, we would discover that one of the raw materials was bad—off quality, off color—and it should have been rejected. And worse—that our own company made the bad raw material—not some outside vendor!

Invariably, someone would have tested the suspect raw material, and it would have failed. Then they would test it again, and again, and maybe the fourth time, it would pass the test, simply because it was a bad test to begin with, and if you do a bad test often enough, sooner or later, everything will pass it. And once passed, it would be sent on to be used, and only when the final product failed to meet its tests weeks or months later, would this huge sequence of rejection, blame, chasing leads, and eventually discovering the root cause would the culprit be found. But by then, everyone would have forgotten about the problem with the only lasting affect being the lingering perception that R&D develops products that we can't reliably manufacture.

I will say that, on occasion, we would do a really bang up job of thoroughly and fundamentally investigating and understanding why a product failed, and make lasting fixes in our raw materials, processes, and tests. And once we fixed a problem with one of our products, many of our other products would also improve. Some of our most sophisticated customers found this to be especially valuable and this earned us great respect and trust. And in the end, we were able to produce a better, more reliable product. Eventually, we would use six sigma methods to make sure that all of our products could be reliably produced.

Ideally, our suppliers and customers would allow us to work very closely with them to improve their processes as well, so that we all could better satisfy the end needs, but this was rare and took a great deal of trust and respect on everyone's part.

If this chapter illustrates anything, it is that R&D and quality, production, sourcing, and sales are deeply intertwined—that we really are one team when facing the customer, and the supplier. Excursions are a way of life in most industries, and catching them, understanding them, and fixing them are important aspects of research and development—our own CSI but without the dead body, with only slightly less pain, and none of the glamor. I will tell you that in each company and industry where I worked, there were a handful of guys that really knew how to do this well, to dig in, to get to root-cause, and to have the knowledge and credibility that gave our customers the confidence to continue with us as a supplier even if we were occasionally unreliable. These guys were often unsung, unappreciated, and were none-the-less vital to the success of the organization. Thank you for saving my bacon all too often.

Lessons learned

1.   New products are fun and exciting and represent a terrific opportunity for companies to grow; but if your existing supply of products or services is consistently off-quality, none of your customers wants to hear about the new stuff.

2.   Chasing down root causes of excursions is a special talent that should be nurtured and rewarded. Instead it is often thankless.

3.   All processes, raw materials, and test methods drift. It is incumbent to design products that can meet customers' needs within the normal range of variation, but it doesn't always happen this way. During the development process, the full range of variation is never fully understood, and sooner or later, one element of the process will drift out of control and cause problems.

4.   Simplicity in design is one good practice. The more complicated the design, the harder it will be to get to root cause when things go awry. Compare a product with ten components to that of a product with only five. Now assume that each component requires five tests to see if it is in spec. Pretty soon you see that the more complicated design can

overwhelm the investigator with potential issues and tests and data. It can be very hard to fish out a root cause with so much going on.

5.   Obviously—never make big changes without telling your customer, and never lie to them. If you do have a potential way of saving money, bite the bullet and share it with them equitably.

6.   If you don't really understand your product and how the components work together, it is impossible to properly specify each of the components. For example, if you really knew that the only variable in fumed silica that mattered to rubber was its surface area, you could set a tight range on surface area, hold your suppliers accountable, and live happily ever after. Sadly— that isn't the case. We would certainly specify the surface area of the fumed silica, but that just wasn't enough to keep it in spec.

7.   Product design and development that fails to consider production, consistency, cost and quality is really half-baked. If there is resentment towards R&D for developing products that can't be reliably produced, then frankly, we often deserve it. And sadly, this happens all too often. Like an elaborate computer program, our products can have bugs that don't get worked out before the customer adopts them, and soon enough everyone is mad at us. This is our shame. But rarely do we have sufficient time or resources to thoroughly vet all of our process, raw material, and testing variation.

Chapter Twelve

Don't Blow a Gasket, Spiro

Gaskets are rubber inserts that are designed to keep engines from leaking. Two faces of metal are machined to approximate flatness, a rubber sheet is inserted, some bolts are tightened and the rubber is squished between the faces and stops any leaks. At least they work until they get chewed up by the heat and oil. Then you get a leak, a messy garage, and an expensive repair bill.

Gaskets are ubiquitous in engines, and silicone rubber is the best material for them. GE Silicones made a lot of money developing and producing unique rubbers for gaskets that were especially heat and oil resistant. It turns out that after engine fluids cook a long time, their chemistry can become harsh and damage the gasket materials, so we developed additive packages to slow this process down to exactly seven minutes after the warranty expires. Then we developed rubber for the aftermarket! Nice business.

One of our customers had cut us mostly out of the process, just buying our raw materials known as gums and fillers, but developing and blending their own specialty grades of rubber to mix and mold and sell to the car companies. Ostensibly, we didn't make as much money selling our raw materials as we would selling finished and compounded products, or so a dumb R&D guy like me would think.

During my tenure as head of GE's rubber R&D group, the customer came forth with a proposal which would get GE to blend their special grades of rubber for them, and sell them the finished goods rather than the raw materials—and all at lower price than they were currently paying for the raw materials!

Naturally our sales team thought this was a great idea. I don't know-- it seemed to me like more work for less pay? But why would an R&D guy even question such logic?

In fact, I thought this was a horrible, horrible idea and was not at all shy about letting the business guys know. Not only would we make less money for more work, but there were some serious and fundamental issues with the dozens of special grades of rubber that this company made. For one thing, their stuff often didn't work. By that, I mean that they would mix up a small batch of rubber in the correct formula. Then they would make a test gasket, measure a bunch of properties as specified by the car companies, and the rubber would fail some of the tests. For example, the rubber might need to not break under a load of hundred pounds, but their batch would break at eighty. So they would take the failed rubber, throw it back in the mixer, add some stuff to make it stronger, then test it again. They would repeat this a bunch of times until they got it to work. The batch would last a couple weeks before they would run out and need to make another batch.

We couldn't do this at GE since our mixers were scheduled out weeks in advance and we also had no way or place to hold the rubber several days during testing, and then if it failed, to transfer the rubber back into the mixer for adjustment. Plus we had no capacity for tweaking on the fly.

The second bad part of this idea is something called crepe-hardening. When you make fresh, uncured rubber, it has the consistency of a Tootsie Roll®- soft and chewy and which can be molded at high pressure into a gasket shape. But after the rubber sits for a few weeks, it crepe-hardens and crumbles more like peanut brittle than a Tootsie Roll®. In other words, you can't mold it and you can't even reblend it. It is toast. Since our customer made small batches which were consumed immediately, they never ran into crepe hardening; but since we made big batches, each batch would have to last months, not weeks, and crepe hardening was a big problem. Not to the salesmen, of course—just to R&D and Production.

And finally, though it might be possible to redesign the rubber formulations to make them capable and with a shelf life, it would require changing the formulations which would take a long development time—at least a full year if everyone in my group worked on it flat out—and would still require a lengthy and costly requalification by the car companies who were loath to change anything.

In other words, if we were to take on this project, it would take all of my resources to work on a project that would end up losing us money, maybe not work, and would preclude my entire research team from working on higher-value opportunities to be used in consumer goods, health care, electronics, and aerospace. Serving the automotive industry was usually the least profitable of any of our customer segments.

So yes, I hated this idea.

It made utterly no sense for us to take on this project, other than the customer was basically blackmailing us by threatening to buy their raw materials from someone else, which would mean a big loss of revenue.

So we had a big brouhaha. I argued vehemently and vociferously against taking on the task of reformulating several grades of low-value rubber, and warned everyone that we would have no resources to take on new stuff for a year. I don't think they believed me. But I was really fit to be tied. The regional sales manager didn't want to lose his sales, and he didn't really care about what happened to the rest of the business.

Finally, our CEO, Dave Cote, intervened. He ultimately decided for us to take on the job because sales were tight that year and he didn't want to lose several million dollars of top-line revenue, however non-profitable it might be.

After the meeting to discuss this project, Dave and I happened to be walking back from the Marketing building together to the headquarters and R&D building which were next to each other, and I really let him have it. We stood out in the parking lot toe to toe, yelling and kicking and spitting like an umpire and a manager do after a bad call, and I told him in no uncertain terms that this was a bad decision and he told me in no uncertain terms that we were going to do it because he couldn't lose the sales.

He won the argument.

Glad he didn't fire me—in fact I think he actually appreciated me fighting hard for something I felt strongly about. I'll say one thing about GE's in- your-face culture- it sure beats the polite Midwestern culture where nobody dares have any conflict, public or private. But still…we took the business.

Do you want a happy ending? OK I'll give you a couple happy endings.

First- Dave Cote left GE Silicones shortly after we took this deal, to become CEO of GE Appliances, then TRW, then Honeywell. I'm sure he forgot about this gasket business two minutes after our argument, and he went off to live happily ever after. Our regional sales manager? He left GE Silicones and went on to a successful career at GE Capital and he never thought two seconds about this lousy deal either.

And for me- I was exactly right—the rubber grades were not manufacturable, and it really took my whole group a full year to reformulate the products so that they barely worked, all at ridiculously low profit margins, some at a loss. And we indeed had almost no resources to pursue new opportunities that were more profitable.

Unwilling to take on assignments I couldn't fulfill, I ended up having to decline so many new product requests that I became known as "Dr. No." After I left GE Silicones and went to the Lighting business, that moniker followed me and every time I was considered for a promotion elsewhere, people would check on me and find out that I was "Dr. No," and I would become a leper. My career at GE was derailed and I eventually had to leave the company.

Lessons Learned

1. Sometimes you need to walk away from business that isn't worth it, even if your measures in the short term will go down.

2.   Sometimes you can do everything you can to stop a bad decision, and still it gets made and you end up paying the price.

3.   Taking on a bad project and then leaving others to hold the bag may be good for your career, but it doesn't make it right.

4.   If your R&D guy says it is more work than it is worth to solve a problem, believe him. R&D guys really want to take on projects so it must be a very bad idea if they don't want to do it.

Chapter Thirteen

Automation for Fun and Profit

During the time that I was leading the rubber R&D group, GE got into six sigma in a big way, as I mentioned in Chapter Eight. Six sigma is nothing more than a systematic way of fixing issues in cost and quality- issues which abounded in the rubber business with its antiquated formulations, aging equipment, and irreproducible test methods.

We were having quality issues with one of our rubber grades- also used in a gasket but for a different automotive company- in this case, an aftermarket supplier who sold repair kits for when the original gasket leaked.

Interestingly, many gaskets were replaced that didn't need to be replaced. Sure there may be oil dribbling out of a gasket, and a shrewd repairman, especially a dealer whose cars are under warranty, might point out oil on the outside surface of a gasket to an unwitting customer, and tell him that a gasket rebuild was needed. But silicones are funny molecules. There is a lot of space between the silicone molecules, and oil will nicely fill up the pores. Gradually the oil will naturally diffuse through the gasket like water in a sponge, and eventually makes its way out to the surface. It looks like a leak, but it is just a very slow, natural diffusion process. The amount of oil loss is negligible and the risk to the engine is also miniscule. But it looks like a leak and unknowing, or unscrupulous repairmen will recommend a new gasket. And as long as the carmaker is paying for a warranty repair, neither the customer nor the dealer will care about the cost since it is billed (for a profit) to headquarters. So the unnecessary repair gets done.

In any case, there was a large after-market gasket business. One of our grades was suffering from quality issues and we did a six-sigma project to try to understand the cause and how to fix it.

Our scientists studied all the key ingredients and processes to make the rubber, and what they found was that one of the fillers we used was especially critical to the performance. On a batch of rubber, we might add fifty pounds of the filler, and they determined that we needed to add this accurate to plus or minus (+/-) a half a pound. Otherwise, the rubber would be too soft or too hard. But when they studied the process for adding the filler, it was only accurate to (+/-) two pounds. In other words, we could never be sure we were adding the right amount accurately enough. As a result, they identified a new way of adding the filler to much higher accuracy and implemented the new process. It worked great and the customer was delighted, as were our Production and Quality departments.

Moreover, by fixing this one product, every one of our products using this new and improved filler-addition-process was also vastly improved, saving the company a king's ransom by improving the quality of numerous grades. This is the beauty of six sigma—you solve a problem once and it propagates and fixes several problems you didn't even know you had.

Six sigma methods are not simple or easy—rigor and care never come cheap and easy, and most people would rather do the quick-and-dirty and move on. Sometimes this works out just fine, but most of the time, it comes back to bite you. If you don't truly understand your product, process, raw materials, and test methods, you can count on something going awry and then you, and your customers, will have a mess on your hands.

I was among the first wave of people trained in six sigma methods, and I immediately saw the importance and embraced the process for its intrinsic value. I was keen to get my whole team trained, but there was a huge backlog of trainees and a shortage of trainers, so we were going to be pushed out well over a year. I felt this was unacceptable, and decided to do the training myself. I arranged for my full group—scientists, engineers, union technicians, our group secretary, to meet one noon hour a week, with union employees paid overtime, lunch provided for all, and all participation being voluntary. Everybody attended.

Having just been trained, and not being terribly strong in statistics, I muddled through the teaching, often with lots of help from the students. It took several months, but we got through the material. And even though the quality of the teaching was substandard, I think everyone in the group really respected the fact that six sigma was so important to me, that I went out of my way to get the tools and knowledge into their hands. Their buy-in was huge. And as a result, my group won prizes for the best six sigma projects for years to come, even long after I was gone, and over half the group became black belts or master black belts, which was the ticket to advancement at GE.

Interestingly, I did not win a lot of friends in the six sigma organization who considered me a rogue. They were not happy that I was unofficially teaching, which was their job. It was also expected that people would actually leave their current jobs and make six sigma their full time job, a notion I did not support. I felt that we should all just do our jobs better, using the six sigma methods. And even though I met all the requirements for becoming a six sigma master black belt including training, teaching, and mentoring projects to successful completion, I was told that I needed to leave my current job and become a full time master black belt to become certified.

It is with deep sadness that I don't have a framed and signed Master Black Belt certificate in my basement, leaving a barren space right next to the Plastics Team of The Year trophy of 1983 and my third-place 2004 golf league plaque.

Lessons Learned

1.   Six sigma is a simple, systematic process for identifying the key variables that really influence the quality of a product or process.

2.   Once you identify the really important things to control, it is usually a simple matter to fix them.

3.   When you fix the problem in one area, it often fixes problems in several other areas where maybe the problems weren't so obvious or severe.

4.   By teaching six sigma myself, my team got shorted in teaching quality compared to the professionals, but their buy-in was huge because it was important enough for the boss to step out and make the extra effort on their behalf. And they really ran with it, making a huge difference in their projects and results, as well as their careers.

Chapter Fourteen

Light Bulbs Are a Blast

After three years at GE Silicones, and having worn out my welcome in the rubber business after getting stuck with the gasket issues I wrote about in Chapter Twelve, I moved on the GE's famous Lighting group in Nela Park- GE Lighting's headquarters in Cleveland, Ohio. The same boss I had at Central Research—Bill Banholzer—had just been named VP of Engineering, and he tapped his old friends, including me, to take on leadership assignments. My new title was General Manager, Halogen Engineering.

Halogen lamps are special versions of incandescent lamps just like the one Thomas Edison invented back in the 1870's. With an incandescent lamp, electricity passes through a highly resistive wire made of tungsten, and the wire gets very hot. In fact, tungsten will get to around five thousand degrees F. Like a fire, all hot things glow and give off light. Tungsten is used because it is refractory which means it won't melt at these high temperatures. What makes a halogen lamp different from a regular Edison incandescent lamp is that the tungsten filament is also sealed in a tiny glass or quartz capsule inside the bulb, one that has been filled with a very high pressure inert gas such as argon or xenon. The high pressure gas keeps the tungsten from evaporating as fast as in a normal incandescent lamp, so that the lamp can go much longer without burning out. Or you can run it hotter which enables the lamp to put out whiter, brighter light for less energy. Because of the high pressure capsule, halogen lamps are over fifty per cent more efficient than regular light bulbs.

For those of you who are curious about why these lamps are called "halogen," halogens are familiar atoms such as chlorine and bromine and iodine. A trace of these is added to the pressurized argon or xenon in the capsule, because eventually the tungsten does evaporate. In a normal incandescent lamp, over time, tungsten slowly evaporates and you might even see a small blackish ring along the base of an older lamp which is the tungsten that has evaporated and condensed on the cooler surface of the bulb. Since the capsule is very small in a halogen lamp, about the size of a fingertip, if the tungsten evaporates and condenses, the tiny capsule gets blackened and pretty soon, no light can escape the bulb. For some reason, many customers who buy light bulbs prefer lightness to darkness; they can be so picky.

The trace amount of halogen in the vapors turns the black tungsten metal that evaporates into a white, transparent tungsten salt, so the bulb stays clear. Also, the white tungsten oxyhalides that form will vaporize and transport back to the filament and re-deposit the tungsten in a quasi-recycling process. Someone in the 1920's figured this out though it took GE decades to figure out how to make it a commercial success.

When Bill Banholzer was given the assignment to lead GE Lighting's technology group, he was explicitly charged by Jack Welch to re-energize innovation there. After years of almost total focus on manufacturing cost reduction, GE's lighting technology had been falling behind the other two lamp companies- Philips from The Netherlands and Osram from Germany. In fact, during Bill's first meeting with Jack Welch at GE's annual leadership meeting held each January in Boca Raton, Florida, Jack pulled Bill aside and told him he had a "blank check" to do whatever it would take to return GE Lighting to pre-eminence. Wow! That doesn't happen very often in an R&D career where begging for money is the norm, as we saw in Chapter Four.

Now a "blank check" from Jack Welch isn't really blank—he just meant that we shouldn't feel constrained by the budgets that were already in place. He would certainly come back to review our ideas and exercise the line-item-veto if they didn't meet his standards.

When Bill returned from Boca that early January, 1999, he immediately brought his staff together to introduce me, since it was just my second day on the job, and also to share the exciting news that we had this great opportunity to invest in new technologies straight from the Chairman, whose main goal was to push the lighting envelope to new and unheard-of limits. And that Jack would be visiting in a few weeks to go over our best ideas. Wow!

I left the meeting all pumped up, and called my new staff together to share the good news. Now these guys were all seasoned lighting experts—every one of them had spent their entire careers at GE Lighting, while I barely knew which end of a lamp to screw in. And naturally, they were a little suspicious and perhaps resentful of an outsider and close pal of the new VP coming in and taking over. But in any case, I was excited to share the good news and to solicit their ideas. After all, for years they had been forced to subjugate their big ideas and only work on cost savings and minor tweaks, and were probably frothing to try something bold and innovative.

After I told them the news and asked for their ideas, what I got was not quite wild enthusiasm....rather something akin to embarrassed silence. Actually you could hear a pin drop. I tried again..."Surely after all these years, you have bold new ideas stashed in a drawer somewhere?" Nope. Nothing. Nada. I guess when you get out of the habit of innovating, it is hard to break back in. This was an extremely low-risk culture where little beyond cost-cutting passed the muster and failure was met with swift punishment including likely termination.

After my initial goading didn't work, I asked "Well what is the competition doing that Jack is so worried about?" Finally someone said that Philips had just introduced "Halogena®" which was a kind of sleek looking halogen light bulb that goes into a normal light socket just like our familiar so-called A-Line Edison incandescent lamp.

As I mentioned, halogen lamps offer some significant advantages over regular incandescent lamps. They cost a bit more, but they last a lot longer, put out much whiter, brighter light, and are much more energy efficient. Almost all the retail stores use halogens in their displays and ceilings for these reasons, and halogens make up a huge fraction of automotive headlamps. The only minor problem is that tiny pressurized ampoule inside. You see, any time you have hot, pressurized glass cycling between room temperature and thousands of degrees, there is a tiny chance of explosion.

But halogen bulbs are always placed inside a big, thick outer bulb like in your car headlamp, or in a spotlight or floodlight, so if they explode, no big deal. But somehow, Philips was skipping the bulky outer shell and just putting the halogen inside a thin sliver of glass just like a regular light bulb. Wow!

So being new and dumb, I asked why we didn't do something like that. I was told about however unlikely, all pressurized halogen capsules have an intrinsic propensity to explode. Yes it was extremely rare, maybe one in a million. But that in no uncertain terms, this particular team wasn't about to risk causing a fire or exploding a glass bulb in someone's face, let alone besmirch GE's impeccable reputation and brand representing the highest standards of safety and quality that was over a century in the making.

Of course—who could disagree? Well....me.

Foolishly, I asked why would Philips be willing to take these chances. Don't they care about explosions, fires, glass in the soup, liability and litigation? Apparently not! They probably figured the risk was worth it— plus they don't sue as much in Europe. And you know those crazy, madcap Dutch—what is human life to them, anyway? It was probably all good fun to them, kind of like Russian roulette!

Hmmm...I wasn't really buying this, but I went along because I was brand new to the group. My guess was that Philips had actually figured out how to make the bulb perfectly safe. As it turns out, their capsules were made of quartz rather than glass which is intrinsically safer and stronger, though costlier as well. And they had figured out a clever way of pinching the filaments to reduce the explosion risk. But we didn't know that at the time.

In any case, I asked if we could somehow make a GE version to be explosion-proof. "Yes" they told me, but the glass would need to be thick, like a Coke® bottle, and nobody would buy such a lamp because it was heavy and ugly. OK- it seemed like a Coke® bottle light bulb was a non-starter. Was there no other way to make it explosion-proof?.

Then I had an idea! I had just come from the silicone rubber business, and I knew that we made some really strong, crystal-clear grades of rubber used in baby-bottle nipples and automotive and oven gaskets. Why don't we just coat the lamp with a barely-visible thin skin of rubber, kind of like a condom? Then if one in a million explodes, you just get a small bag of broken glass that you toss, but no explosion, fire, sexually transmitted diseases, or glass in baby's crib.

This group of dedicated and experienced engineering managers, having spent their entire careers working on halogen lamps, were immediately and wildly enthusiastic about the idea. I could tell because of their dead silence and expressions of derision, in between scowls and muttered comments about how dumb this idea was. OK maybe they weren't all that enthused and just needed a little persuasion.

So I spent the next week, all the while the clock ticking as the Chairman's visit rapidly approached, trying to find anyone on the technical or commercial side to warm up to the idea. But this was a stubborn lot. Nobody budged. They universally hated the idea of a silicone-rubber-coated lamp for a myriad of reasons—safety, manufacturability, cost, market acceptance, risk of failure just to name a few.

It looked as if a once-in-a-lifetime chance at a blank check from Jack Welch, the "20th Century's Greatest Business Leader" (according to Time Magazine) was going to go uncashed, at least by the Halogen Team. Even worse— how could I stand before the Chairman and say "I'm sorry sir, but we have no ideas in halogen," especially after my boss brought me in expressly to re-energize innovation.

Please- just shoot me and put me out of my misery.

As our old girlfriend "desperation" began to rear her ugly head yet again, I became panicked. I finally brought the cross -functional team together and admonished, "Look—I can't go to the Chairman and say we have no ideas. This is mass suicide. We'll all get fired. So I have no choice but to present the rubber-coated halogen A-line project either with you or without you. I am perfectly willing to tell him that I am the only one who wants to pursue this idea and that you all think I am crazy, if that is what it takes. And I promise you that if it doesn't work, I personally will tell them that you all objected, and I will take all of the blame."

With this fairly grave threat, they very reluctantly signed up for the project. I think this is the only time I had to resort to coercion and shame in my entire career, but hey—desperate times call for desperate actions.

Our finance guys quickly got to work and did an analysis of the project— calculating development and capital and production costs, sales volumes and estimated prices and product introduction timing—and when all was said and done, this project looked like it would lose money hand over fist! Cool beans, Spiro—you come here out of nowhere, rock our formerly comfortable world, and we'll show you how dumb you are! This project of yours is DOA- Dead on Arrival!

So I pushed back hard on every assumption. Could we not find used equipment somewhere in one of our warehouses? Could we not charge a few cents more? Could we not cut the cost a hair? What if we sold a few more and a few months ahead of schedule? Once you realize all the assumptions that go into these fancy Net-Present-Value (NPV) calculations, you learn that they can be tweaked at will, provided you can get the finance guys to go along. They are usually very reasonable people, especially if you say something sweetly persuasive like "Karl—I would hate to tell the Chairman that this is a great idea, but Karl in Finance won't go along because he is afraid of a little risk."

So the financial calculations were done and redone until finally, at the eleventh hour, the project actually eked out a meager profit, assuming everything went perfectly, of course. But the volumes that Marketing would commit to were low, the development costs were high, the timelines distant, and the starting sales date was far enough into the future that perhaps everyone on the team was hoping at least they would have enough time to find another job before the day of reckoning. But for the moment, we moved ever so slightly from deeply in the red to almost black figures...shall we call them faded gray—sort of the color of an unidentified body several days too long in the morgue? Hooray! And at least I would be invited to the dance. Getting funded by Mr. Welch was overwhelmingly out of the realm of possibility, but the halogen group could at least avoid the shame of showing up completely empty-handed and devoid of creativity.

Unsurprisingly, of the twenty-plus projects being presented to the brass, who now included Jack Welch, along with GE's Chief Technology Officer Lonnie Edelheit, GE Lighting President Dave Calhoun, and about a dozen other VP's and GM's, my little project came in dead last in terms of payback—so far behind the pack that it was almost an embarrassment to present. At least it was last on the program since the projects were racked and stacked and presented in order of projected return on investment. Maybe we would really get lucky and they would run out of time and not even get to mine.

The day of reckoning arrived, and as us lowly paeans waited outside the meeting room, my boss went through the presentations one by one while we waited for white smoke to emerge from the rooftop. During the breaks, we heard that things were not going well. The ideas were neither big enough nor bold enough. I was really dead meat.

Alas, they got to the end of the twenty projects in time, and the laughable rubber bulb got its day in court....and to everyone's surprise, THEY LOVED IT! Lonnie Edelheit, my old boss from Central Research, said that this was a real winner, and Jack told Lonnie it was about time—that "R&D hadn't done a thing with the A-line light bulb since Thomas Edison." Not only did they love it, but they also wanted increase the volume ten-fold and shorten the development time to eighteen months. Wow. Glorious! We were heroes. My boss, and his, were thrilled. Wait until I tell my team! They will be so happy. We were on the map.

I quickly called my team together to let them know the great news—not only were we fully funded, that our project came out with flying feathers, and not only were we approved, but that the Chairman wanted us to ramp up the volume tenfold and cut the development schedule in half.

These guys were so thrilled, that they were speechless! Well OK, they were speechless because they were basically afraid to tell me what they really thought—that my idea was stupid, couldn't be done, was going to waste a ton of money, put them all in the spotlight, and get them all fired. And worse, not only were they on the hook for an impossibly bad idea to begin with, but now it was even worse because the volumes were massive, the timeline shortened, and they were suddenly moved from comfortable obscurity to the center of the Chairman's microscope! Ouch.

Somehow, I was not gaining in popularity. I can imagine what they were thinking, but wouldn't dare print it.

Of course I could tell they were shocked and dismayed and overcome with fear. But what could I do? It was now a *fait accompli*. So I did what good managers do—assigned people to the project and charged them with coming up with tasks and a timeline. And I put my best and most experienced guy in charge of the project.

Two days later, we had our first major planning meeting, and he showed up with a timeline that was twice as long as what we were allotted, and costs that were quadruple, still ending with volumes and costs that didn't begin to approach the target. He basically said the project couldn't be done. I asked him to sharpen his pencil and try again.

A couple days later, he came back and told me he was quitting the project and transferring out of the group. At least someone had brains in Cleveland those days.

Three other guys assigned to the project also came up to me the next couple days and said they were transferring out of the group, as well. I guess they didn't believe in the project. You think?

I wondered if I could transfer, as well. Maybe GE has a research station in Tierra del Fuego. Here I was, less than a month on the job; I had been forced to commit my group to a completely untenable project and was creating a mass exodus. Not bad for a start, but what could I do for an encore?

As I sat in my office contemplating strategies, along with correcting typos in my resume, one of my new employees politely knocked on my door. In came a very thoughtful and senior Hungarian engineer named Laszlo Lieszkovszky. Laszlo had joined GE a few years back when GE had acquired Tungsram, the Hungarian lamp manufacturer, and was one of the few Hungarians to emigrate to the US in order to be closer to the action. Laszlo had been a senior manager at the time, but came over as an engineer and individual contributor in order to learn the ropes and prove his worth.

Laszlo said just one thing to me: "I can make your project work."

If there was ever a moment in my life when I felt like I was down to my last friend, this was it. "Yes, you can have the project!" I told Laszlo, without any hesitation. I will never, ever forget Laszlo's courage. Thank you forever.

Remember that in a halogen lamp, there is that tiny glass capsule that gets very very hot—thousands of degrees—but in our plan, this sits inside a much bigger light bulb, a thin glass bulb just like the ones you use day in a day out. Our plan was to coat the outer bulb, of course, because nothing would survive the heat of the inner bulb.

Three major parallel tasks were the most urgent—one was to figure out how to assemble the inner halogen capsule inside a normal light bulb glass, using sophisticated robotic equipment to make all the seals, welds, and electrical connections. GE was very good at this sort of thing. The second was to learn how to coat the outer light bulb with silicone rubber so that it looked good and worked to perfection. We had zero experience here. And the third major task was to test the assembly and prove that together, they would contain the explosion.

I quickly contacted my old group in the rubber business and had them send us all sorts of our clearest and toughest rubber grades which presumably we would just dissolve in a solvent and dip-coat the outer bulb just like you might dip a wick in wax to build up a candle. Meanwhile, Bob Berki – one of our engineers—developed a foolproof method for making our halogen light bulbs explode on purpose. And finally, Laszlo knew of some well-used, somewhat antiquated robotic equipment in Hungary that we could have— the kind that was used to assemble glass halogen bulbs used in automotive headlamps. He made some calls and got it for us.

Since I was the silicone expert, I was least worried about the rubber coating process. Of course, I was utterly and completely wrong about this assumption. But what else is new?

To begin with, the coating process worked horribly. When we dipped the bulb into the rubber solution, we got wrinkles and bubbles, sagging and slumping, orange peel, drips and spills, and the coating was neither uniform nor good –looking. And if that wasn't bad enough, none of the coatings held up when they were exploded. None! It seems that I had made a fairly major miscalculation. You see, silicone rubber is indeed very, very strong at room temperature, but the surface of light bulbs, even the outer shell that is far from the capsule, still gets very hot—a couple hundred degrees or more. And rubber gets quite weak when it gets hot. Oh dear— major *faux pas*, Spiro.

There was another minor problem with the silicone rubber coating. When it gets hot, it not only gets weak, but it also decomposes. And when it decomposes, it not only gets even weaker, it also gives off formaldehyde…you know that toxic stuff? The stuff they preserve dead bodies with? I wondered if there was enough formaldehyde to preserve my dead body, because surely this was where I was headed in short order.

Luckily, I remembered that my rubber group had worked on a project to make silicone oven gaskets, and we had developed a special additive to make the rubber more heat resistant. I got some of this and actually, it seemed to work. We might explode some glass is in peoples' faces, but at least we wouldn't poison them. I am feeling better by now.

Still unable to make a nice, uniform coating, I contacted one of my old pals who ran a silicone molding business up in Racine, Wisconsin. They mostly made medical devices, but when I explained my problem, they thought they could help. Their plan was to take the glass outer bulb, clamp it inside a metal shell that was ever so slightly larger, and do a process known as "overmolding" in which the liquid rubber would fill up the shell, cure in a matter of seconds, and out would come a coated light bulb. It was a nice idea, but it failed badly. It turns out that no two glass bulbs are exactly the same. In fact, they vary in length and diameter by several millimeters. So most of the time, when they closed the metal shell onto the glass bulb, all they got was a lot of broken glass. Oops. Just another small miscalculation on my part. But then again, when you have to invent a breakthrough project on the fly, you can't really think of everything.

At least my rubber gaskets weren't exploding like the ones on the Space Shuttle that killed a bunch of astronauts; here we were just killing a few light bulbs and a bunch of careers—mostly mine.

Meanwhile, one of our engineers, Bill Walters, had gone into a lengthy study of how to make very uniform, perfect coatings, and discovered the ideal prototype- the condom! I kid you not. I wonder how the folks in Purchasing felt when we bought a condom machine. You might think they had a good laugh. But then again, you know how to get a Purchasing Agent to laugh tomorrow? Tell him a joke today.

Our "Little Dipper," after a thorough and systematic six-sigma experimental design by our terrific engineer, finally produced a fantastic and consistent process for coating glass bulbs that was indeed clear, uniform, and beautiful. And they were free of bubbles, bumps, drips, sags, tears, and all number of flaws that you can only imagine. I guess the condom people don't like to have too many failures, either.

And boy these coatings were tough, tough, tough! Of course, they still didn't contain the explosions, but let's not get greedy. After all, we still have a few months before drop-dead date. Plus, some very good friends of mine had recently left GE Silicones to start their own specialty silicone company, and we had hired them to develop a very strong rubber for our lamp application. Surely the best minds in the business could succeed where I hadn't. They tried a bunch of stuff and kept us apprised of progress for several weeks. Then all of a sudden, we stopped hearing from them. And they stopped answering our calls and e-mails. Finally after weeks and weeks of trying to get ahold of them, I got the word—they fired us! Ouch. And we were the customer! Now what?

OK I was beginning to get seriously nervous. Luckily, my molding buddy from Racine called me up with a suggestion. It seems that breast implants were all the big news—this was around 2000 and Dow Corning was in Chapter Eleven bankruptcy and was facing major lawsuits over leaky breast implants. My pal heard of a new silicone rubber that had been developed for breast implants that was really tough to make certain it would never, ever leak. I ordered some right away; we developed a coating process; and finally, well over a year into the process- we had our first success. Thanks to condom and breast implant technologies, one of our coated light bulbs exploded, and the little baggy of silicone survived! It worked! Once...but if it worked once, maybe we could get it to work twice or even three times. Of course, the bulb was also cold. When we ran the lamp for an hour to get it good and hot, the silicone weakened and we got glass everywhere. Rats.

Back to the drawing board—but through even more experimental design, multiple coatings, and adjusting the heat additive- Laszlo and his team got the process to work. Hot, cold, and every time. We did it! It looked beautiful and it really worked.

Sure we had some bugs to work out. A lot, in fact. But at least the major principle had been proven-- that we could reliably make a rubber-coated halogen lamp that would safely contain in the unlikely event of an explosion. My new boss – Michael Idelchik- was excited. Michael had replaced Bill Banholzer who had moved on to GE Plastics as VP there. Michael even decided to put the new light bulbs in his office as a showcase. Cool. And he was pushing me and our business VP- John Krenicki who is now Vice Chairman at

GE—to accelerate the launch of the new product. I pushed back, saying we weren't quite ready, and though they went along, I could tell they were disappointed. You know us conservative R&D types and our science projects.

I have always been an early bird- normally showing up at work by 6 AM to get an early start before the multitudes pour in with their issues *de jour*. So it was a good thing I was in my office just before seven a.m. the very next day (I kid you not!) following Michael's and John's push to accelerate the commercial introduction of our new lamp. I could tell this was no ordinary morning when Michael called me urgently, saying, "Please come quickly to my office—your light bulbs have exploded and my desk and chair are on fire." He had no sense of humor about it. I guess there really were a few bugs, after all. In any case, how many people do you know who can truthfully say they exploded their boss's office and didn't get fired?

Of course, we needed to prove that it really worked all the time, and our safety guys were a tough bunch, as were the lawyers. So our next task was to build and operate a rack that had thousands and thousands of prototype lamps. Laszlo had thousands of lamps made up, and we literally lit up the roof of the engineering building with these rubber- coated lamps. It was so bright that moths began arriving from distant countries for tropical vacations. Of course, halogen lamps normally burn thousands of hours, so it is hard to get a lot of failure data in a hurry, but after months of continuous testing, a few actually did explode and every one successfully contained the broken glass. Now as a consumer, this limited test data might not make you feel terribly comfortable, but there is a branch of statistics known as Weibull failure analysis, in which a very few failures can predict how the multitudes will behave, and based on these data, we were given the go-ahead to proceed to commercialization.

Now at this point, we had spent hundreds of thousands of dollars. We could still walk away from this project, lick our wounds, and move on without costing the big GE very much. The real money comes when you build factories and have huge launches and marketing campaigns. Now the serious horse trading began.

Our first issue was that the inner bulbs were made in the US, the assembly equipment was in Hungary, and the VP of manufacturing wanted to do the coating in Mexico, along with using the project to pay for some nice new offices and labs there. I think in Congress they call this "pork barrel," but in any case, we managed to make whatever deals we had to get his, and everyone else's buy in. Sales and Marketing agreed to pricing and monies to roll it out and to develop pretty packages; safety got some new test equipment; it seemed that when it finally became time to write the big check, everyone had their hand out. But despite all this, we got it done— we got every VP's signature including Engineering, Legal, Safety, Manufacturing, Sales, Marketing, Finance—and our *Opus Major* was finally ready to go to our new business president Mike Zafirovski for final approval. Wow we did it! Thank you team; thank you Laszlo. Nothing could go wrong now….right?

Wrong. Surprised? I didn't think so.

"Zaf" was on his way out the door as I brought in the Plant Appropriation Request (PAR) for his final signature. He said not to worry-- he would be back in tomorrow and would sign it then. No problem. He just had a little personal business to take care of. That little personal business was merely for him to resign GE and become president of Motorola! No Zaf, no signature. Oh well, just have to wait for the next guy to come along. At least the heavy lifting was behind us—what would a few days matter in the grand scheme of things?

Matt Espy was named as the next president of GE Lighting and would arrive in a few days. Surely he would recognize a terrific project like this.

Being a Sales guy at heart, Matt's first instinct was to go meet with our best customers- Home Depot and Wal*Mart. From what I gathered from the rumor mill, not missing an opportunity to take advantage of the new guy, the retail behemoths pushed him hard on price. My understanding was that Matt didn't budge enough with Home Depot, so they fired us on the spot and decided to line their shelves with Philips, instead. Wal*Mart wasn't so rough; they happily took a price reduction and kept GE as their main brand. Welcome to the light bulb business, Matt.

So by the time Matt returned to Cleveland having been on the job just a few days, GE Lighting was basically broke, having lost one major account and significant price at another. Now hard-pressed for cash, Matt put a hold on all new investment projects including—you guessed it—the rubber-coated light bulb.

As a recession soon hit, the rubber-coated halogen lamp, a *bona fide* leapfrog in cost and performance, never saw the light of day.

And truly it never will. The juxtaposition of an overcapacity of halogen bulbs from the headlamp segment along with some free assembly equipment now long-since scavenged for parts, were keys to making the economics work. These have forever passed.

At least my impeccable record of commercial disasters remained intact.

I would say the cancellation of this project—so bold, so visible, so fraught with risk and pressure, so many obstacles successfully overcome—was one of the saddest moments in my career. But I will also say that my boss went out of his way to give significant cash bonuses and personal words of appreciation to everyone involved. That was real class and not many companies reward a good loss like GE, and it certainly made me proud to work there.

A couple post-scripts. In the interim while we were developing the rubber coated halogen lamp, we actually did launch what we lovingly called "The Coke® Bottle"- a regular looking frosted light bulb with a small halogen capsule inside a thick, heavy bulb. It was pretty cool and the sales were modest but not bad, as I recall— certainly more than enough to pay for the extra development costs of the rubber lamp. Also, now a decade later while perusing the shelves of Home Depot, I happened to see that GE Lighting is now selling what looks like an exact copy of the Philips Halogena®. I'm sure there are subtle difference, but it looks basically the same. So whatever Philips did to solve the safety issue, GE somehow figured out how to emulate it, and now both companies sell a halogen A-line lamp that is longer lasting and more efficient than the incandescent lamps of yesteryear. As far as I know, nobody has been killed by Halogen® explosions. And luckily, this is part of the GE product line because recently several countries including the US have outlawed the sale of incandescent lamps because of their low energy efficiency.

Lessons Learned

1. As you might have noticed, Bill Banholzer became my boss not once, but twice and would yet again a third time. In a lengthy study of what makes a successful career at GE, the million-dollar consultants determined that the surest way to the top is to attach yourself to a rising star. In this case, Bill was the rising star and he brought me along. But don't get me wrong—you still need to deliver the goods or the star will drop you like a hot potato. It is actually quite a good symbiotic relationship that works to everyone's benefit.

2. Certainly the most important lesson I learned from this story was that every single day, every single moment counts. Just think if we had done one extra experiment or saved just one day along the two years adventure. Just maybe, Zaf would have signed off the plant appropriation request before quitting, and we would have built the plant after all.

3. I made many bad assumptions—that we could successfully coat the lamps and that they would contain an explosion. I forgot that silicones are strong when cold, but weak when hot. And worse—that they actually decompose to form toxic vapors. These are some pretty serious failures in thought. And yet, by taking on what seemed like a bunch of insurmountable problems, the guys on the project came through and somehow made it work. Never underestimate the ingenuity of our technologists. Give them the impossible and just maybe they will come up with

great things—perhaps different from what you planned, but none the less important.

4.   Courage and leadership have nothing to do with titles and organizational charts. Laszlo Lieszkovszky had more courage than a hundred guys with fancy manager and executive titles who spend more time afraid of failure and covering their butts than in really trying to make something bold and risky happen.

5.   Borrowing technology from cross disciplines is often the surest way to innovate. Here I just happened to transfer from the rubber to the lighting business— what an odd jump indeed, and yet by combining the two, we really did come up with something novel. And of course, why not throw in condoms and breast implants just to make the story a little spicy.

6.   Again we see how important networking is. Thank goodness for my friends at Limtech in Racine for first failing to overmold the lamp, but knowing enough about what we were trying to do to identify an alternative solution, and then going out of their way to let me know of this new, extra tough rubber. Nowadays, we call this "open innovation" which is to share your problems with vendors, academics, and even competitors, and hope that someone comes up with a solution, regardless of where it comes from.

7.   You know—for the people that jumped ship early on in the project, I completely understand. For them, maybe late in their career in a culture where failure wasn't tolerated, it was asking them too much to go so bold.

8.   It is really tough to be a new leader, coming in from the outside, and obviously a crony of the big boss and having no knowledge or experience in the field. But then, to be forced to make a major innovation in such a short time- it is little wonder I generated so much resistance and hostility from my guys. I didn't

have the luxury of a "First Ninety Days" to get to know them and find out their needs and help them succeed. This was such an unusual confluence of events and I know I put the Halogen team through a lot. I'm sure that many of them still harbor anger and resentment toward me. My style has always been to shut up and listen and learn at first, and then take action, but sadly, I couldn't here.

9. If you want people to really innovate, it takes practice and encouragement. Failure cannot be punished, but rather, rewarded. This is a concept that parents of infants seem to know instinctively while teaching their babies to walk and talk and eat and dress, but they seem to forget this the moment they get to the office.

10. Experimental design is a systematic process for identifying the key factors that influence results. Our guys executed experimental design to perfection in developing attractive and tough rubber coatings.

11. It is vital to develop accelerated testing. If we didn't have a device that would reliably and deliberately blow up the bulbs, we could never have developed coatings that would contain the explosions.

12. Weibull statistics are a terrific way to determine product life cycles, even very long ones like locomotives, after only a very few failures.

13. If you are new on the job, it is probably a good idea to get the lay of the land before you go and visit your really biggest customers, even though we all truly believe that there is nothing more important than keeping our really big customers happy.

14. Taking big chances is actually exciting and fun and you learn a lot. And the consequences of failure are probably a lot less than you think. I mean, if the worst thing that can happen is that you get fired,

what the heck? It's a lot better than living your life in fear and obscurity.

Chapter Fifteen
The Easiest New Product

Sometimes, you work very hard on a new product development, and it still fails. I think by now you are beginning to see that this is a pretty common theme in the R&D world. According the Robert Cooper, one of the foremost experts in new product development, less than ten per cent of ideas make it through the development stage. Even more seriously, over a third of new products that have gone through the whole nine yards— ideation, research, development, scale up, manufacture, and commercialization—still fail to recoup their costs. The odds of bringing a new product successfully to market are stacked way against you.

And then again, sometimes you get lucky. The Halogen UltraXL® was one of those easy ones – a product that took almost no work and sold like hotcakes.

It is a sad fact of incandescent and halogen lighting that most of the energy gets wasted—well over ninety per cent in the case of your typical Edison lamp. You may recall that all hot objects radiate. And that the tungsten filament in a light bulb gets very hot—enough to give off visible light—that nice golden yellow that looks like the sun. In fact, all hot bodies, such as the sun or a bonfire, give off radiation with a characteristic color associated with its temperature. Over ninety per cent of the radiation from incandescent lamps is infra-red, not visible. Infra-red light is what makes a fireplace so warm. Sure the flames are a romantic splash of visible flickering yellow and orange and blue light, but by far, the bulk of the radiative energy from a fire is infrared. And unfortunately, the human eye doesn't see infrared. You are probably familiar with night-vision goggles like you see on TV. These are clever electronic devices that detect infrared radiation, and then use electronics to make it visible.

In the late 1980s, when I was working at GE's Central Research Department (CRD), some of my colleagues there, along with researchers at GE Lighting, in Cleveland were developing a fabulous new kind of lamp that actually recycles the infrared radiation that is otherwise wasted. They took that tiny halogen capsule that we read about in the last chapter, and shaped it into a parabloid which is a fancy word for an egg-shape. They then stretched the tungsten filament right down the center. Finally, they coated the bulb with something called a dichroic mirror, a series of fifty alternating layers of tantalum oxide and silicon oxide that had the unique property of allowing all the visible light to transmit, while reflecting all the infrared light back to the filament, which was driven by the parabolic shape. The layers were deposited to nearly atomic perfection without cracks or flaws, and they were remarkably designed to adhere when cold and extremely hot, because that little capsule gets well over a thousand degrees when the lamp is running. When the lamp was turned on, just like a regular halogen lamp, some fifteen per cent of the energy came off as visible light—the kind of light people pay for. But in this special lamp, the infrared light was now reflected back to the filament, making it hotter. Since the filament was already hot enough, we were able to turn down the electric power, and still get the same light output. So in the all-important measure of lumens (light) per watt (power), the lower power made this lamp really efficient, saving around fifteen dollars of electricity over its lifetime.

This lamp, known as the HalogenIR®, was a real breakthrough. It won "The Best of What's New" award from Popular Science in 1990, and a decade later, none of the competition had been able to figure out how to make anything like it. This lamp was truly a breakthrough in energy efficiency and gave GE Lighting pre-eminence in this particular genre of lamps.

The physics of incandescence dictates that there are three interdependent variables—the amount of light a lamp puts out, its energy efficiency, and its life. Moreover, Nature allows us to get two out of three. For example, for a given lamp, you can run it hot—which makes it efficient in terms of light output, but it also burns out fast. The reason it burns out is because you evaporate tungsten from the filament, and eventually the filament gets so thin that it breaks. If you can run a lamp at lower voltage, it doesn't put out as much light, but it lasts a lot longer because the tungsten doesn't evaporate as fast. Maybe you noticed that if you run a lamp turned down just a bit with a dimmer switch, it seems to last forever. That's true.

Whenever we developed a new lamp, we usually made three versions- a hundred-thirty volt, hundred-twenty volt, and a hundred-ten volt. Most American circuits run at one-twenty volts, while in Japan, they are closer to one-ten or one-hundred even. But some circuits, especially those located nearby power plants, for example, are operated on circuits that are closer to one-thirty volts, so we routinely made some tweaks to the filament design to produce special one-thirty volt lamps.

Some of our professional lighting contractors knew that one-thirty volt lamps, when run in one-twenty volt circuits, would last a lot longer. They wouldn't exactly put out the brightest, whitest, most efficient light—but they would last two or three times as long as the regular lamps. And most people wouldn't see the difference in light quality or output. When our contractors had a fixture in a hard-to-get place like a church ceiling, they would use the one-thirty volt lamp in a one-twenty volt circuit, knowing it was hard to replace.

Based on what we learned from our contractors, our engineers and marketing guys decided to "develop" the Halogen UltraXL—a lamp designed to last much longer than the regular lamps. All they actually did was take the one-thirty volt lamp that was already on the shelves, and package it in a one-twenty volt box. Yes it put out fewer lumens and fewer lumens per watt, but it lasted a lot longer and for some places- this was exactly what the customer wanted.

Now here was the real beauty of the "invention." Around the year 2000, the US government had established energy efficiency standards for light bulbs. If you ran a regular one-thirty volt halogen lamp in a one-twenty volt circuit, you would lose about ten per cent of your energy efficiency— enough for all of our competitors to fall below the energy efficiency standards. What a shame. But because our halogen IR lamp was so energy-efficient to begin with, we alone were able to achieve the energy efficiency standards even in a down rated bulb. As a result, we had a unique niche product—one that lasted much longer for especially hard-to-get fixtures.

The customers loved it. It sold like well and got GE lamps some much- needed shelf space in Home Depot. It won a prize for the best new lamp at Light Fair—the annual convention of light bulb people. And it really required little R&D—just a new box with the new ratings for light output and energy efficiency and life.

One of the things us R&D people are measured on is sales of new products. Another measure is called "vitality index" which is the fraction of sales from products less than three years or five years old. This Halogen Ultra XL really helped my scores, even though it took almost no work. Hey-sometimes you get lucky.

Lessons Learned

1. Sometimes, you already have a great new product sitting on the shelf that had been developed but for one reason or other, never made it to the marketplace, but suddenly due to changes, its time has come.

2. Even better are new products which are "AKA's" or Also Known As.

    You may already be selling the product for one application, but in an entirely new application, you can give the product a new name and sell it for more money. A dirt-cheap adhesive used to attach shingles, for example, all of a sudden finds a new home in the medical or aerospace industry and can command a much higher price. Just make sure you don't sell it as "Elmer's Glue" in the standard squirt bottle; put it in a sophisticated new package and call it "Space Adhesive" or "Biocompatible Adhesive," and mark it up nine hundred per cent. Sure the customers can go to the trouble of trying a bunch of stuff designed for other applications to look for cheaper alternative, but more often than not, they will pay a premium for their "unique" application, whether it really is or not.

3.   Know your physics. In this case, we knew the tradeoffs between lamp life and efficiency as a function of voltage, and this allowed us to identify a niche.

Chapter Sixteen

Go East Young Man

It was around 2000, and globalization was in full swing. There was already an onslaught of cheap halogen lamps from China that were populating the shelves of Home Depot and Wal*Mart. And while the big brand names of GE, Philips, and Osram truly offered a benefit in performance, lots of people bought on price alone. As a business, we decided, if you can't beat them, join them. Our goal was to have a "Good, Better, and Best" line of light bulbs, with the former two outsourced from low cost countries such as China, and sold under the GE label. Presumably we would help our Asian partners with improved design, materials, testing and assembly in order to meet the rigorous GE standards of performance, quality, and safety-- all at a substantially lower cost than the main brand that was manufactured in the US.

I brought this up at one of my staff meetings early during my tenure as Halogen Engineering GM, and I was met with derision. Over their "dead bodies" would they put the good GE label on some cheap Chinese knockoff. It is never easy, is it? But to me, the handwriting was on the wall—we needed to outsource lamps at a lower cost or we would eventually lose our share and our shirts in this very price-sensitive arena.

One of the biggest critics to this idea was Denny Lynch—a terrific and seasoned engineering manager who had spent his career at GE Lighting and had forgotten a lot more than I'd ever know about halogen lamps. Like all of the team, Denny cared a great deal about the quality and safety of our products and the value of the GE brand. And he was not about to sacrifice decades of building the brand on some cheap Asian knockoffs. And he wasn't shy about telling me.

So I did the unthinkable—I put Denny in charge of the outsourcing project.

Not only did Denny hate the idea, but he also had a couple bad knees— probably from some old football injury. I'm pretty sure Denny played ball somewhere and I know he was a diehard Fighting Irish fan. The last thing he would ever want was to go on long flights to Asia cramped on a plane in uncomfortable seats with bad knees for fifteen hours, then traipsing across rural China kicking about a bunch of sweat-shop lamp assemblers, all the while eating and drinking God-knows-what. I am sure he cursed me the whole way there and back. And he ended up making several trips—some of which I joined him. Now to me, I just love exploring exotic places like rural China, eating scorpions and snakes and drinking Mao-tai, but I'm the oddball, I know.

And we truly saw numerous shops that were indescribably bad. There were often very young girls assembling lamps– they looked like they were eight or nine years old, though their papers always said they were sixteen. And the heat was unbearable with little or no ventilation, no safety glasses, people welding and soldering with burns all over their hands and arms. And the lamps themselves were atrocious-- they probably wouldn't last five hundred hours while ours were rated at three thousand hours. It was all terribly discouraging.

After several trying trips to Asia—Denny was finally able to find one group in Taiwan that turned out to be terrific. They had some manual assembly and some automation; their work conditions were excellent and their quality matched. With some investment and training and the addition of some critical GE components—this group was able to make excellent lamps, lamps that even Denny was proud to put the GE label on. And their costs were half of ours. GE was able to have a good-better-best strategy and keep our shelf space in Wal*Mart and Home Depot with a combination of home- grown and outsourced lamps.

Lessons Learned

1. Globalization is the way of the world. It makes fine political fodder to try to fight out-sourcing of American manufacturing jobs, but in the end, consumers want the best value for their buck and will not pay a penny more than they need to. If the product comes from a low-cost country- so be it. It is far better to learn to be competitive in a global world than to try and fight it, because inevitably, the best value will win in the marketplace. We found that by joining forces, we could offer a full line of products with differentiated costs and performance. It was a win for everyone.

2. By putting the most vehement critic of outsourcing in charge of the project, I was sure that it would get done right without compromise, or it wouldn't get done at all. And I wasn't any more willing to sacrifice the brand than anyone else on the team.

Chapter Seventeen
Personal Transitions

In most R&D careers, there are transitions. Some technologies evolve, and individuals evolve with them to sustain their careers. Others end abruptly as a result of politics, economics, and advancement. Certainly, if you were an expert in color photographic film working for Kodak in 2003, you found this out the hard way. If you worked in aerospace, you also did not likely experience a soft landing.

During late 2000, GE Lighting came on tough times as a result of the economy and transitions in the lighting industry. We had a significant cutback in R&D investment and personnel, and being a lot more fungible than most, I decided to leave the Lighting business in order to save a few more jobs there. GE had just decided to acquire Honeywell, and I was needed to kick the tires on the potential acquisition—formerly called "due diligence" and "integration."

Due diligence means that you dig into the details of the acquisition to make sure that you are buying what you think you are with no surprises.

Integration is putting together a plan post-merger for what you keep, fix, sell, and how the new company will operate as one. For a big multi-billion dollar deal like Honeywell, this was no small task. My role was to look hard into Honeywell's materials businesses and especially their R&D in these areas. It was a blast getting to learn about whole new areas to me— electronic materials, fluorines, nylon, wax.

But when all was said and done, what seemed like a personal vendetta between GE's CEO Jack Welch, and the head of the European Economic Union Mario Monti- now president of Italy— quashed the whole deal.

I was left without a job. I was offered a nice post in the GE Plastics' facility in Mt Vernon, Indiana (we affectionately called it "Mt Vermin"), but at the same time, I was courted to become VP of R&D for Nalco in Naperville, Illinois—a subsidiary of the French multinational utility Suez- the same folks that built the canal. It was a really big job, and it was excruciatingly hard to leave GE after nearly 22 years. Despite my grumblings in the last few chapters, I really loved working at GE and had the highest respect for Jack Welch. I also felt that I would be giving up a great deal of job security and a rich pension down the road. But I also doubted I would ever get to become a VP at GE. I ultimately decided that I would rather try my hand as a company officer, leading a large and complex global team, even if it meant less money and security. It was time to move on.

Lessons Learned

1.   From a career standpoint, R&D in many ways is really not much different than other disciplines. As an individual contributor, a scientist or engineer can continue indefinitely with progressively complex or significant projects. Similarly, in Finance, Safety, Business Development—great individual contributors are needed and can make great, fulfilling careers and lives. But once you get on the management ladder, it is up, or out.

2.   There really are more important things than money. If your career is stalled, sometimes you need to change organizations rather than live frustrated for the rest of your career.

Chapter Eighteen

French Management is an Oxymoron

One of the main functions of leading an R&D organization is to make sure that your employees are working on the right set of projects. We call this set a portfolio. We have already seen examples of several individual projects that I worked on. Now as VP of Nalco, I was charged with being the steward of our entire portfolio.

You can cut a portfolio of new product/process research projects in many ways: risk, reward, timing, industry and segment, geography. My approach has been to work closely with the appropriate business leaders, especially Marketing, to understand which projects will pay off the most— while making sure there is a good balance among the various kinds of projects. For example- there are smaller new products called derivatives— usually requiring a small modification of an existing product line to reduce cost, improve performance, or extend to new applications. Derivatives take a few months, usually, and are almost sure to successfully sell, since customers are already buying your current version, and have usually asked for a refreshed product that they also plan to buy.

The next kind of project is a platform—usually involving a new process, a new customer, or something bold with step-out performance. Platforms often lead to many patents since they are highly novel and offer competitive advantages. There is likely already a market for the product, but we don't happen to serve it, just yet. New platforms are higher risk and take longer to reach fruition—often more than a year. But the platform is probably well within the current business scope, and if the targets of cost and performance are met, it will probably sell. The last set of projects are called breakthroughs, they are really new, and very high risk and take a lot of patience. But they can payoff big. I think the first iPod and iPad are examples of breakthroughs. I always liked to keep a few of these breakthroughs going, but the bulk of my projects were in the derivative and platform areas. Also, a major portion of R&D's portfolio is consumed in firefighting issues for excursions in product quality, as well as manufacturing productivity, and sales support including customer adoption. These can be unplanned, and are bottomless pits.

I always kept a close finger on the pulse of projects, and actively managed the portfolio to optimize impact while matching people and skills to projects. It is what an R&D director does for a living. However, the French took this to new limits.

The executives at Suez would establish an earnings target—say six per cent for the following year. This would somehow get divvied among their various businesses. For example, perhaps Nalco got a seven per cent target. Then each of the projects would be given a sub target such that the sum of all of the projects would add up to the seven per cent. Exactly. Not 7.01 per cent.

So far this sounds reasonable, though in reality, one project will inevitably exceed its target and another will fall short; as long as the total works out, everything should be OK. Or so you would think. But not with the French.

Still not enough, each project would be given a research component, and schedules, milestones, and personnel would be allocated to each project. And the personnel needed to match the output—one would not put three people on a project that would pay out less than a two-person project. So you would need to move one person from the three-person project to the two-person project to make it work out properly.

And it was not enough that the sum of people-projects would add up to the total number of people in R&D; that would be too simple. Each specific individual would need to be allocated to the tenth of a person-year to each of several projects such that each of the individuals was exactly allocated one hundred per cent.

Only when every project was fully resourced to the correct fraction of people-years, and each individual, by name, was allocated exactly one hundred per cent, was the exercise complete. And of course, R&D was just a small part of the total; all of the projects would be fully resourced with the right amount of commercial, research, manufacturing, quality, and finance people such that one hundred per cent of each employee in the company was fully allocated and each project delivered exactly the right amount of money to the company coffers at exactly the right time. Then we were done with the planning process.

A handful of people worked full time on the planning process, while the rest of us worked like mad during the planning period to populate these vast arrays of notebooks and spread-sheets that accumulated the people-project-hours-outputs. And the brass at Suez would scrutinize these notebooks to make sure that everyone was fully allocated and it all added up. And finally, once the notebooks were given the seal of approval, they would go on the shelf and never be looked at again.

And then the real business of work would begin, and as usual, it would scarcely resemble anything that was in the notebooks. And at the end of the year, if you somehow managed to beat the numbers, you were heroes, and if you missed, you were goats. *C'est la vie.*

Lessons Learned

1. A research department has a portfolio of activities that should reflect what the business needs. It is important for the organization to ensure a good balance of risk and reward, segment and geography, cost cutting, quality improvement, and growth.

2. Planning processes are established with the best of intent- to ensure that the resources are properly

allocated. However, most planning departments, and especially the French, run amok with this process. Far better is to focus on placing capable, and motivated individuals in leading roles, give them the broad outlines of scope, and trust that they will maximize their impact. And hold them accountable for achieving their targets.

3.   "The best laid plans of mice and men..." often go awry, said the great poet Robert Burns. In the war of R&D, there is ongoing triage, with customer quality issues from excursions taking precedence. Often the best new product developers also have a lot to offer in understanding and correcting product failures. It is a difficult decision to take someone off of a growth activity such as advanced product development, and have them firefight a quality issue. Oh and of course, even if resources are suddenly reallocated to meet crises, you are no less responsible for the new product developments that were scheduled as part of the planning process.

4.   Resources in R&D are only modestly fungible. A chemist may indeed be able to support a breadth of chemical projects, but a biochemist will have trouble getting up to speed on a paint project. A physicist may be adept at mathematics and the fundamentals of electricity and magnetism, but might not readily plug into a circuit design project. Very broadly capable individuals are rare, but are priceless in affording resource swings when needed.

5.   Things are constantly changing for R&D. Customers' needs change, the competitive landscape switches, quality and manufacturing issues abound, suppliers come and go, prices adjust, and people come and go for several reasons including regime change within the organization. Sadly, R&D is buffeted by the changes, which happen in time cycles that are much faster than the

development process. It is little wonder that R&D will appear out of synch with the businesses—it always is! How could a business that is run by quarterly earnings and quick market intelligence and customer whims come anywhere close to matching the lengthy product development cycle? It is the great challenge of R&D leaders to sustain programs and continuity under the constant barrage of immediate business needs and short-term thinking.

6. Certainly a key to success for the organization is to have a robust, growth-oriented new product pipeline. It is little wonder that innovation gets so much attention, as critical as it is to the overall future of the company, and even more so, the greater the technical content of the enterprise. In my experience, elaborate planning processes do little to facilitate growth, and often accomplish just the opposite by hogtying leaders who may be held accountable for goals that are no longer relevant, and certainly employing resources in bureaucratic exercises instead of working on their projects. Far better is it to have adept and motivated leaders who are held equally accountable for both near term and long term success, and who are trusted and left to focus on their mission.

Chapter Nineteen

Patents and Intellectual Property

The last time I looked, I have been issued twenty US patents, and about twice that number from around the world. You would think that I am a big supporter of the patent system, but I am not.

To the layperson, a patent is a really big thing. It represents an official document issued by the government that grants you exclusive, monopoly rights to produce your invention for a period of time—generally under twenty years. It is also an official statement that the government recognizes your invention as novel and an improvement over whatever else is out there. And for this, you pay a pretty hefty fee.

I recall with some sadness, a friend who had developed a new kind of glove. She paid nearly ten thousand dollars to a firm to get her idea patented, and she really has little hope of getting any of this money back. I would bet that the sum total of value she will get from having the patent is an engraved copy of the patent, framed on her wall, and perhaps the ego boost and cocktail party stories that go along with it.

A patent explicitly claims what the assignee actually owns, and how the product or process works. By law, you are required to describe the invention in great detail. In principal, anybody could read your patent, and make an exact copy. But selling that copy would be illegal, and so ostensibly, the inventor is protected.

On the other hand, if someone were to make an exact copy of your patent and went about selling it, you would have some pretty expensive prosecution on your hands; patent fights start in the millions of dollars and go on up from there. Are you ready for that? As a private individual who made some new kind of glove, do you have that kind of money? I doubt it. Moreover, in describing exactly what you did to make your invention, you also describe exactly what you didn't do, and clever individuals are more than capable of coming up with design-arounds—ways to capture the essence of your patent without explicitly violating it.

If you have patented a process, this is even harder to defend, because if someone is practicing your process behind closed doors, you will need to have some pretty strong evidence before you can get warrants to prove it.

Big companies can often afford to defend patents, and some huge awards have grabbed headlines-- for example RIM's Blackberry and Apple's I-phone core patents are valued in the billions of dollars. But most patents are never practiced and even fewer defended.

Some regions of the world don't necessarily value intellectual property in general, and specifically patents. While at Cabot Microelectronics, a Korean company produced a copy of one of our patented products. I have no idea what was said or done in the patent litigation in Korea, but I do know that when all was said and done, the competitor was still freely practicing our patented technology. Courts would naturally tend to favor their citizens, don't you think?

But even in the United States, we had a patent on a catalyst which we put into water to make one of our polishing compounds work. An American competitor took the same catalyst, adsorbed it onto a solid, and put the solid into the water. They claimed the same catalyst adsorbed onto a solid was different, though we held the belief that, once they put it into the water, it simply desorbed from the solid and behaved the same as our catalyst. A multi-year, multimillion dollar suit took place, and a lay jury sat there listening to our experts saying it was the same, and their experts saying it was different. Many of the jurors probably never even took high school chemistry. Who the heck should they believe? In the end, they compromised by saying that our patents were still valid, but the other guys weren't really infringing. So basically all our legal machinations did was enrich a bunch of lawyers.

My feeling is that the best defense of a market is to have the best products and service, best costs, and quality, solid supply assurance—and to continually keep ahead of the competition by developing generations of new and improved products that customers really want. Hopefully by the time a patent issues, now delayed by several years because of the backlog in the patent office, you will be long onto the next, and second-next generation of new products. So why spend the big money defending a patent for something that is already outdated by the time it issues?

That being said, companies, legal departments, R&D departments, and inventors have a vested interest in sustaining the system. When I arrived at Nalco, it seemed that people just submitted patent disclosures, and they were filed on an *ad hoc* basis with little strategic thinking behind it. Someone might ask, "Does the invention work?" and someone else might ask, "Are we selling it?", and if so, or even "maybe someday," the patent would file. And filing those patent applications was not cheap. Sure the filing fee was around a thousand bucks, and the inventors got a few hundred dollar bonus as well. The cost of the lawyers was already borne by the company, but realistically, it probably took ten thousand dollars worth of a lawyer's time to write the application. And then if the patent actually issues around the world, the cost of translating the patent and globalizing the applications and maintenance fees runs up to two hundred thousand dollars per patent! Not chump change, especially for an R&D manager who had to fight tooth and nail to hire a technician for forty-five thousand dollars a year.

To combat escalating intellectual property costs, I introduced a patent review board at Nalco, led jointly by Marketing and R&D. Randy Fortin, my Marketing counterpart, had the brilliant idea of displaying a digital thermometer on the screen during our review meetings—the kind you might see as part of a fundraising project for the

United Way or the State University Alumni Association. Only with this thermometer, each time we approved a new patent application, and decided in which countries to file, the thermometer would shoot up thousands, tens of thousands, or even hundreds of thousands of dollars. Randy would say things like, "Folks, you just spent four hundred thirty thousand dollars." This visual exercise really got people thinking about the cost and value. Pretty soon, the "ego" filings all but disappeared, and only the most salient and core patents were pursued.

Frankly, the best inventions are often kept as trade secrets. Especially if you think that copying the invention will be difficult. If patents are not going to be respected or enforced, trade secrets are usually the best way to go. The next time you hear of a start-up who proclaims their vast patent portfolio, you might look askance. And when you hear someone brag about how many patents they hold, or even how many publications they have in the technical literature, ask them if any of their inventions are actually making money somewhere, and then stand back and listen to the silence.

Lessons Learned

1.   I'm sure that patents have their place, protecting inventors and companies from intellectual property theft. But beware that often, it is those very patents that open the door for outright theft in countries that don't necessarily respect intellectual property, or to clever design-arounds that are expensive to prosecute, and which lay juries might find difficult to comprehend.

2.   Patents, and publications, are false proxies for legitimate innovation and company valuation. In the end, I believe that real innovation results in an item of commerce that someone pays actual money for. I know this is harsh, and I don't want to denigrate the real fundamentals of science that comprise the vast bulk of technical literature. But frankly, it is astronomically easier to publish or patent

something, than it is to commercialize something new. I cannot recommend enough the book, *"Wrong – Why Experts Keep Failing us..."* by David Freedman. The author shows how the vast majority of published technical literature is (how to put this delicately ?) simply inaccurate and incomplete. If you took every conclusion in the technical literature and assumed the opposite was actually the truth, you would be more likely to be right. As a rule, not the exception, published data are biased, the interpretations are self-serving, and the intrinsic systems of peer review are badly flawed. Read Freedman's book for a sharp splash of ice water in the face of science.

3.   The dollars involved in patents and IP are staggering- on the order of thousands to file a patent application, but quickly reaching seven or eight figures in a defense. Even merely globalizing a patent gets you over a hundred thousand dollars pretty quickly. And really, how much good is a US Patent in a global economy?

4.   Often, the best ideas don't get patented, but are protected by trade secret. If you have hard-to-copy technology, this may be the best way to go.

5.   In general, with the enormous backlog is the patent examiner's office, you may well have commercialized two or three generations of advanced products before your patent issues. Do you really want to spend valuable resources defending yesterday's technology? In my opinion, you are better off saving your intellectual property dollars, and investing them in new products, better customer service, more reliable supply chain, and improved product quality—things that customers actually care about.

Chapter Twenty

3D Trasar®

Almost all industrial processes require water- processess like papermaking, petroleum refining, chemical and food processing, and so on. Nalco makes a nice living by treating process water with chemicals to prevent scale, corrosion, and fouling. Let me briefly explain what these are.

With scale, the minerals in the water precipitate out and coat pipes and valves and things. Maybe you have seen how your hot-water heater gets filled with minerals from hard water. This is the same thing that happens in a big way in major process industries. Nalco and its competitors have developed a bunch of chemical additives to keep this from happening.

With corrosion, the chemicals in the water will pit and etch and gradually rust and dissolve the pipes and components in the process stream. Maybe you have seen how the acids in Coca Cola will dissolve a penny. Various natural and added chemicals in the water can corrode the process equipment, so again Nalco and others have developed chemical additives to prevent this from occurring.

Fouling is a biological phenomenon. Microorganisms grow in water, consuming natural and added chemicals in the process and leaving a biofilm along the surfaces that can affect the function and performance of the system that is fouled. Again, Nalco and others have strategies for keeping microorganisms under control. You probably know someone who owns a swimming pool, and goes to great lengths to keep it clear and clean with an arsenal of chemicals and test kits. The same thing takes place in water-based industrial processes.

So at Nalco, among other things, we developed and sold additives to control scale, corrosion, and biofouling. But each customer's system is unique in temperature, flow, size, concentration and so on. A power plant does not have the same duty cycle as a refinery, a macaroni factory, or a toilet paper production line. So not only did Nalco provide treatments, we also provided expertise—"The Man in the Can." Literally tens of thousands of "water-doctors" working for Nalco who would go out to our customers, each of whom runs an industrial process. The water doctor would examine the system, take samples, test things like pH and concentrations of various salts and ions, and then make a recommendation of what treatments to use. The customer would then buy these chemicals, put them to use, and for a few days—everything would be copacetic. And then, inevitably the system would crap up and the customer would scream at the water doctor, and he would scurry over, and make some adjustments that would hopefully improve things. For a while. Then the seasons would change or the process would change, and things would crap up again. Or maybe nothing would change, but it would still crap up. That's our world.

Understand that these are never closed systems. Water is always being evaporated or spilled. Old process water is sent down the drain and fresh water is always being added. And the additives to control scale, fouling, and corrosion are being lost or consumed at various rates. Even if the water doctor miraculously added exactly the right amounts of chemicals at a given time, a day or two later, something will have changed and the system will go out of whack. Guaranteed. Being a water doctor is a job with high job security, but it comes with a lot of personal abuse. Sadly, the water doctors were generally flying blind, never knowing what was actually in the system.

Then along came John Hoots, a PhD chemist whom Nalco hired right out of the University of Illinois and long before I got there. John had the great idea of adding a trace amount of fluorescent dye with each batch of scale inhibitor and then measuring its concentration with a flourimeter. He reasoned that even if during the operation of the industrial system, some water was added and other water was lost — that the amount of dye left in the system would still indicate the concentration of the additive that was still left in the system. It might not seem like much, but at least now, for the first time, our water doctors had a pretty good idea how much scale inhibitor there was in the system at any given time.

It turned out to be a big breakthrough, and Trasar® really put Nalco on the map. It was highly protected with patents that competitors actually respected for the most part, so nobody else could measure their inhibitors with the accuracy that Nalco could. And Nalco developed on-line flourimeters so that the water doctors and plant managers could monitor their scale inhibitor levels from the comfort of their homes, or at least, control rooms. Nice.

Then along came NM Rao and a big team of chemists and engineers, who decided that they could develop an advanced type of Trasar®. In their vision, there would be sensors and controls that would automatically measure the scale as it formed, and add just the right amount of scale inhibitor at exactly the right time —along with a second system to automatically measure the biofilm as it formed, and automatically add just the right amount of biocide at exactly the right time—and a third system to measure the amount of corrosion taking place, and automatically add exactly the right amount of corrosion inhibitor at exactly the right time. In principal, the system should run perfectly, automatically controlling scale, corrosion, and biofouling and replacing the water doctor with science. And it would save lots of money by never adding too many chemicals that would be wasteful, and most importantly, never risk having too little treatment, a situation that could shut the plant down or reduce its efficiency. Brilliant.

And it works!

OK- Not perfectly, but still it is way better than just having a water doctor come out every few weeks and take Strictly Wild Assed Guess (SWAG) or Seventh Planet Estimate (something pulled from Uranus) on what chemicals to add.

3D Trasar® was taken successfully from concept to commercialization over a period of several years, and time has shown it to be a big success. And to a certain extent, the early days of the project happened on my watch as VP. I was a big champion of the 3D Trasar® and made sure it was on the top of my list of priorities. I give all the credit to Rao and his team of scientists and engineers, and only mention my peripheral role to illustrate that there are lots of ideas and projects out there that come from the creative minds of our technical staff. And that an important role of technology leadership is to separate the wheat from the chaff, recognize good projects, and to champion, advocate, and nurture them through their various twists and turns to commercialization. And I assure you, if the project is big and bold and impactful enough, the project will have many critics and periods where somebody big has to hang his neck out far enough to keep it going.

One interesting postscript to the project—as 3D Trasar® was coming on, the traditional Trasar® which only addressed scale control, was becoming obsolete. My CEO, Christian Maurin from Suez, called me into his office and asked me to explore ways to monetize our Trasar® patent portfolio including licensing the older technology. It seemed like a really good idea to me, and I got together with one of my favorite sales general managers to identify a low-risk way of dipping our toe into licensing Trasar® in a small market to see if it was really worth it, or if it would become disruptive. Mike quickly found a partner in his Pittsburgh region who agreed to keep the license small and contained, and the royalty stream seemed to be significant and worth a try.

At a leadership team meeting involving all the VPs and CEO, I presented the plan, fully expecting some concerns. But having addressed the issues of risk and containment, as well as possible damage to the brand, I felt that with the support of the CEO, we would get some traction. And then, we would see how it worked out- would the revenues from licensing offset the risks and possible loss of business?

After going through the details, to my shock, the CEO got up and glared at me, pointed a quavering finger in my direction, raised his heavily accented voice, and angrily questioned, "How dare you risk damaging our business by giving away our core technology." Again, this is after he specifically asked me to do exactly this. I was shocked. Did he forget? Of course not. Sadly, these kinds of Machiavellian manipulations are rather characteristic of the French management style. At least many of my colleagues who have worked for French companies have so told me. We never did follow through with licensing our obsolete technology.

Shortly after that, Nalco was auctioned by Suez to a group of private equity investors from Apollo, Blackstone, and Goldman-Sachs. What followed was a fascinating palace coup in which the leadership team split into two factions, one led by the French CEO and the other led by the American company president. Both factions were vying to run the new enterprise subsequent to its divestiture from Suez. There were even a couple double-agent individuals who tried to play both sides against one another in hopes of landing no matter who became the winner. As you might guess, I was squarely behind the American president, who was eventually the successful leader of the new enterprise. And though I was on the winning side, I was still let go, along with almost all of the VP's, in order to delayer and cut costs. I'm sure my getting sacked had little to do with my performance or character, and I left with fond memories and nice parting gifts.

Lessons Learned

1. Turning "experts," in this case, water doctors, into "expert systems," replete with sensors and controls, represents a significant opportunity for R&D to combine knowledge and technologies to achieve better performance at lower cost.

2. Research and technology leaders don't have to be the guys with all the big ideas—there are lots of creative scientists and engineers and business people to lead the charge. But a very important role of the R&D director is to create an environment

where ideas can thrive, and most importantly—to know which ones to support. The R&D leader needs to have credibility, cross-functional relationships, heart, courage, tenacity and good judgment, in order to pick, sell, and drive the projects that will really win.

Chapter Twenty-one

The Enabling Team

When I arrived at Cabot Microelectronics (CMC) in 2003 as the new VP of R&D, the company was in transition. We had a new CEO, Bill Noglows, who had just replaced Matthew Neville, CMC's founder. Matthew is a brilliant Ph.D Chemical Engineer from MIT, and he did a remarkable job starting, nurturing, and growing Cabot Microelectronics from a small division within the huge Cabot Corporation, to a spun-out public corporation traded on NASDAQ and worth close to a billion dollars. But like most start-ups, there becomes a time to say good-bye to the founder and get more professional management. This time was late 2003.

I was Bill Noglows' first new hire, having interviewed with the older management before he had even been announced as the new CEO. R&D was in a state of utter chaos when I arrived. The former head of R&D was also a brilliant scientist and industry expert, but who rarely ventured outside of the office, I was told. And she had been gone for almost a year. In the interim, R&D had been operating under "seagull management"—you know where the brass flies in, makes a lot of noise, craps on people, then flies away!

Cabot Microelectronics was, and still is, the semiconductor industry leader in the critical technology called CMP- Chemical Mechanical Planarization. CMP is the process to polish the semiconductor surfaces to near-atomic perfection—necessary to deposit layers of nano-scale circuits to connect the transistors.

When Bill Noglows and I and the others he brought on arrived on the scene in late 2003 and 2004, Cabot

Microelectronics was showing signs of vulnerability. Serious quality issues were plaguing the company, and we were about to get fired as a supplier to Intel—the industry leader. Our new products were poorly designed and were difficult to manufacture and use with any degree of reliability. Now don't get me wrong, our polishing compounds were doing extraordinary things—polishing computer chips to near atomic perfection, necessary because a scratch or ripple or debris on the surface just a few dozen atoms thick could cause a short or open circuit and ruin the chip. But with each new generation of chips—something that happened every two years-- the requirements for perfection grew and grew, and we were so busy trying to fix the last couple generations of products, that there was little progress developing the next. We were at a tipping point, where our business was not sustainable without a serious change. The Board understood this and brought in Bill, and a new team to follow, including me.

I spent the first several weeks on the job talking to everyone—employees in R&D, sales, marketing, customers, suppliers- and began to get a good feeling for how grim things had become. We were organized by a half dozen product teams, and virtually everyone on the product teams was busy firefighting production, quality, and application issues. Our old products were failing, and the cupboard was bare of new stuff.

Oh, and R&D was being blamed for most of the company problems. Nice. Welcome to CMC, Spiro.

Based on my getting the lay of the land, I decided to break the R&D product teams into three new teams. The first group became "Engineering," and their focus was to be quality, cost, scale-up, and would include the pilot plant and testing. Yes our firefighting effort was going to be cut, but this engineering sub-team would be fully dedicated to making our existing products work. I brought in some new leadership here. The second group was the traditional product development team, now cut down by two thirds, but focused entirely on new stuff and unencumbered by firefighting and quality issues. The business teams were distraught because they felt I was cutting their staff by two thirds. The third group I called "The Enabling Team," and their job was to get us back out in front of the curve, identifying new molecules and particles and processes for polishing by delving deeply into the physics and chemistry of polishing surfaces. They were put in place to restock the shelves with new core technologies that would allow us to compete in the years to come. The business really hated this group because they felt that if we didn't fix the problems of today, there wouldn't be a future to worry about. I have heard this mantra many times throughout my career.

I assigned the Enabling Team leadership to Jim Dirksen, a scholarly, almost professorial type of individual with deep technical knowledge and broad credibility within the company and across the industry. Jim relished the assignment as he was one of the loudest voices for change within R&D. Jim's technical substance served the program well in ensuring that only projects of significance were undertaken—those that would not only move forward our knowledge base and repertoire of raw materials, processes, and metrics—but also those which would have the broadest customer and commercial impact. Still, he knew he would be under great scrutiny regarding what others might consider to be "science projects."

As I mentioned before, if you want to make an R&D leader fume, just accuse him of supporting "science projects," you know just undertaken for the amusement and education of the research employee. There are no science projects in industry, but this is a very effective pejorative suggesting that the projects will never have any impact. The Enabling Team got this in spades, and sadly, Jim's communication style often exacerbated this perception.

The best part of being the new guy is that, despite objections, you can really make changes—big ones. Obviously, the new guy is brought in because the old way wasn't working. As the new guy, I given a lot of latitude to make changes and to fix things. And I had the complete support of CEO Bill Noglows and a phenomenal Board of Directors, who intrinsically recognized that we were going to fall off the cliff soon if we didn't make changes. The Enabling Team was one of these changes that encountered resistance but managed to stick.

Indeed, within a few months of Bill's and my arrival, Intel did fire us, and our stock crashed from a once high of nearly eighty to something in the twenties. Competitors were springing up all over the place, and our customers—frustrated with us as their sole supplier—were more than happy to help them supplant us. We learned humility fast.

Then something happened. The Enabling Team, put in place for long range purposes, quickly caught the attention of our leading edge customers. The Enabling Team was exactly what they wanted and expected from the industry leader—to take bold moves and become the thought leaders in this technology. And none of our smaller competitors had the scope that would allow them to have anything like this. The Enabling Team was immediately welcomed and embraced by customers, who brought them in for open "R&D- leader- to- R&D- leader" discussions where they opened the kimono on their more distant visions and worries. And in an unexpectedly short order, the Enabling Team began to make a difference. A new particle here, a new additive there, and the shelves began to get repopulated for our product developers. Our tungsten polishing compounds made a breakthrough; our copper products became competitive. We had new products for specialty surfaces. Thanks to similar strong new leadership and bold steps in Operations and Quality, our costs and quality also started to improve. By the end of 2004, it felt like we were starting to turn the corner.

And with the benefit of hindsight, things really did turn around. Yes the competition heated up and the customers leverage dramatically increased. Our prices dropped precipitously but through a combination of new products, quick customization, improved customer service, manufacturing productivity and quality, and a strong drive towards globalization (next chapter), our products, relationships, and reputation improved. Today, Cabot Microelectronics continues to lead the industry, not only winning back some of Intel's business, but also winning five of their prestigious "Preferred Quality Supplier" awards over the last six years. And despite lower prices, by developing concentrates, tunable platforms, and high margin specialties, reducing waste and better managing our suppliers, Cabot Microelectronics sales and profitability are at record highs.

Lessons Learned

1. When things aren't working, bold changes may be necessary, and it often takes someone new and from the outside to move the needle in a big enough way. Insiders have vested interest in the old system and may even be blamed for the current malaise.

2. New leaders have a rather narrow window to make bold changes, before they get stale and tarnished. If you make big changes too quickly, before you have established credibility, your actions won't likely stick. It is important to take the time to really survey the landscape and get as broad a constituency to weigh in on what is needed. You may not act on everyone's input, but people who believe they have been listened to are more likely to embrace changes even if they didn't initiate them. And conversely, people who feel unrepresented will resist changes. Somewhere between a month and six months is a reasonable window to develop plans and begin implementation, in my opinion, and we often hear of the first ninety or hundred days as pivotal. There is an intrinsic drive for action in most good leaders, and it may be hard to not jump-the-gun and try to make wholesale changes too early, even if they are obviously needed. Often the new leader's supervisor will be pushing for a series of actions, as well. It may not be possible to delay certain moves, especially in personnel matters where there is resistance to change. In some cases, the

platform may be burning and the luxury of time is not afforded the new leader. But if you have the time on a new assignment, especially if you are coming from outside the organization, take it and use it effectively by driving for the best ideas and the broadest acceptance.

3. Although we had severe quality issues, and were also way behind on new products, I still pulled back in both of these areas to support a longer-range outlook with the formation of The Enabling Team. I felt it was necessary to restock the shelves for the long term, completely unanticipating the immediate benefits of gaining better customer access through their top R&D folks. Moreover, I was even more surprised that the investment in long term research had an immediate beneficial effect on our current generation of products.

4. If you have the support of your CEO and Board, it makes all the difference. At the beginning of my tenure at CMC, it was necessary to make and drive big, disruptive changes. The fact that we got some early traction and wins gave me enough credibility to keep going and thrive for so many years.

5. In many companies, there are several business teams, perhaps organized around product, market, or region. Often, each business unit has its own, independent R&D team. In some cases, there is also a central research team that may be the equivalent of Cabot Microelectronics' Enabling Team, with their eyes on longer term innovation and seeking synergies across business units. Bold innovation takes a lot longer than product upgrades and redesigns, and most business units and business leaders haven't the patience, and are not incented to resource these projects; the added cost cuts into their profits and bonuses and they are unlikely to be around to reap the rewards of lengthy

innovation. And they have little tolerance for technology risk. All too often, short-sighted views of R&D and technology investment eventually come back to haunt the organization as competition makes major leapfrogs in cost or performance.

Some organizations, ones that can't afford central R&D and divisional R&D, struggle between having a single, centralized R&D organization or several divisional R&D organizations that report fully to business units. I feel that, with good leadership and accountability, the power and efficiency of a single, centralized R&D unit is vastly superior to several independent divisional R&D units. Centralized R&D offers the greatest opportunity for agility, cross-learning, and enough independence to protect projects and people from being buffeted by the ebbs and flows and whims of the marketplace and business managers. A business manager who only cares about making the next quarter earnings target will have little patience for investing in two or three-year projects. Nor is he likely to have the knowledge or credibility to effectively lead a technology team.

Even worse is an organization with only divisional R&D, but with a single, independent chief technology officer, or CTO, who reports to the CEO. Generally, the CTO's role is to try to influence the business managers and divisional R&D, presumably with the authority that comes from having the CEO's and Board's ear. This sounds good in theory, but in practice, the CTO generally struggles for relevance, and at worse, may appear to be underfoot to the divisions. Companies, always seeking ways to control costs, may jettison the CTO during hard times.

Chapter Twenty-two
Globalization of R&D

During the 1990's and 2000's, the semiconductor industry became distinctly Asian-centric. Intel, IBM, Micron, and TI were, and still are leading American chipmakers, but Samsung became a huge force, especially with memory chips, and Taiwan Semiconductor (TSMC) and United Manufacturing (UMC) became huge foundries that produce chips designed by "fabless" chip companies. Japan's semiconductor industry was already strong as the millennium turned, though it was actually showing early signs of decline. Today, about three-fourths of the world's chip volume comes from Asia. And we were located in Aurora, Illinois. Aurora really could not be much further from our customers, and it was impacting our business. We had established production in Japan, but within Asia, Japan was not considered a low-cost country, and our extremely cost-conscious customers had trouble believing they were getting the best value from products developed and made in America and Japan.

Upon my arrival to CMC, there was a strong push to establish a lab in Asia. There was a big debate whether to go to Taiwan or Japan, and in the end, we decided on Japan for a variety of reasons, some right and some wrong.

We worried about protecting our intellectual property and some people thought Japan would be safer than Taiwan since intercompany movement was less common in Japan. We had existing infrastructure in Japan that would make it easier to build and supply a new lab. And to some extent, we were more worried about losing our Japanese customers than we were enthused about gaining Taiwanese customers.

In retrospect, it would turn out that there was more upside in Taiwan's growth than in Japan's decline, but it certainly wasn't obvious in 2003.

Frankly, as much as I wanted us to be in Asia, I was also very concerned about the added cost. I felt that staffing two labs would cost a lot, with the added facilities, depreciation, travel, and materials impacting my budget. I was concerned that we would have to cut back about fifteen or twenty experienced people in the US to pay for the added costs and the ten inexperienced folks we would hire in Japan; and that was not a trade I was prepared to make at such a critical juncture in our company's history. But I was reassured that this would be additive to my budget. And only in time, as the folks in Japan became more experienced, would we offload some work from the US and reduce costs. So I went along.

Within months of commissioning the new facility, we had a recession in the industry, our sales plummeted, and my budget got cut. In other words, in a roundabout way, my worst fears were realized—I was stuck with an inexperienced group in Japan that was largely unproductive, but this staff was untouchable, and I ended up having to reduce experienced domestic headcount by double the new heads in Japan to make the budget, exactly as I feared. Oh well— too late now.

The Japan team got off to a rocky start. We were able to hire a renowned Japanese scholar and industry expert late in his career, who would give us instant credibility with Japanese customers and who would train the new crew. But the hope of this group developing meaningful new products was never realized as they were below critical mass. On the other hand, we had built some terrific new labs with polishing equipment and leading edge metrology, and in time, the Japan team became leaders in polishing process and measurement—two keys to successful growth in new products. And they represented strong lines of communication with our Japanese customers who felt that CMC was more than an American company, that we were Japanese as well. The Japan team never really made big inroads with Korean or Taiwanese customers as we had hoped, but all things considered, I am glad we made the investment as is the rest of the business, I believe.

Meanwhile, Taiwan semiconductor manufacturing really boomed and we were nowhere there. We decided to look for acquisitions in Taiwan, but for an acquisition to occur, so many things needed to line up that this strategy seemed doomed. The best candidate to buy was Epoch Chemical, and they were already tied up with our leading competitor and really couldn't do anything with us as a result, even though we maintained cordial relationships with them.

So we decided to start a small lab in Taiwan, and as in Japan, we hired a senior professor of CMP who was revered by our Taiwan customers many of whom who had studied with him. We also hired the head of engineering for a leading Chinese chipmaker to build our team. And while this small cadre of technologists represented a good focal point for communication with our Taiwanese customers and with headquarters in turn, they were also nowhere near critical mass to be able to develop new products on their own. And the investment in Taiwan R&D was under constant scrutiny.

Our big breakthrough in Taiwan came when, after four years, Epoch Chemical became frustrated with their partnership with our competitor, and opened the door for us to step in. Our country manager at the time had gone to great lengths to nurture this relationship and it finally paid off.

Epoch became a part of CMC and now we had a major laboratory and trained personnel right in the heart of the leading chip making country.

Integrating the Epoch labs into CMC went extremely well, thanks to a companywide integration effort that encompassed everything from IT, finance, sales, and production. Within just a few months, things were operating smoothly, though expectations for the Taiwan team to be quickly developing new platforms across all of our product lines were unrealistic. The best thing that Epoch brought us was access to the key Taiwanese customers and speedy response to customer requests. We quickly leveraged Epoch by combining their capabilities with CMC-originated products, raw materials, process, quality, manufacturing, testing—to present a new, improved face to the center of our world. It has been an overwhelming success.

In addition to polishing semiconductors, we also provided polishing technology to hard-disk-drive manufacturers. We called this the Data Storage group. Our customers were initially located in the Bay Area of California. And like so much of the tech world, they moved to Southeast Asia, especially to Malaysia and Thailand. It became apparent that we needed to move our Data Storage manufacturing and R&D to Southeast Asia as well, and we chose Singapore. Here our decision was very clear—we would hire ten people for R&D in Singapore; they would come to the US for several months of total-immersion training; they would then return to Singapore where they would be on their own; and all the American employees would find new jobs elsewhere in the company, or leave. A small number of the American data storage employees chose to leave the company, but most welcomed the opportunity to train the new bunch from Singapore, and then move on in their careers.

It is simply not possible to start a lab this way and expect it to go smoothly. You cannot impart a lifetime of knowledge in just a few weeks. Indeed, when the umbilical cord was cut between headquarters and Singapore, the business suffered with a sharp decline in progress developing new products along with inadequately addressing quality issues. But the business stuck with the strategy, and I would estimate that in two to three years from its start, the new data storage team was fully up and running independently, and doing well. And while our customers were not initially happy with the transition, the close proximity to their leading supplier and the new local design and support capability offset any hard feelings, and today the business is thriving. I for one, am certain that, had we not moved lock-stock-and-barrel to Southeast Asia when we did, we would have no data storage business today.

And finally, as I was winding up my career at Cabot Microelectronics, Korea was also really booming. It would surprise few people in the industry if Samsung soon became the largest chipmaker in the world, supplanting Intel. And naturally, our sales team in Korea and our Korean customers made it clear that, if we wanted to be successful there, we also needed to be there. And be there we are. By now you know the drill—build a lab, hire a very senior expert, add bunch of people from customers, suppliers, and universities, bring in a few expats to staff the place, go through some growing pains and learning curves, make some missteps and mistakes and most likely, in two or three years—we will see some positive impact. All the while, keeping open to the prospects of local acquisitions that can really jumpstart the program.

From the time I started at CMC to the time I left nearly eight years later, we had added four new labs-- in Japan, Taiwan, Singapore, and Korea, and about a third of our employees were living and working in Asia. And despite having four new labs with all their expenses, the overall R&D budget never went up appreciably. Our effectiveness did go up, in my opinion.

One of the keys to the successful global transformation was to ensure that each location had unique capabilities and roles. These were not satellite labs that were extensions of headquarters; they were on the hook to deliver unique products and services. These labs gave us speed and open communications with our local customers.

I was pleasantly surprised that communication and cultural barriers were not limiting. Everyone from around the world went out of their way to communicate across time zones and language barriers, and never lost focus on winning as the key objective. Sure there was occasional friction and fear of job loss, but we found ways to put these behind us. I give special credit to the key R&D and business leaders in each region for ownership and accountability for making their groups relevant and effective.

Lessons Learned

1. Globalization of R&D is necessary as customers are increasingly global. If you aren't near your customers, they won't be your customers for long.

2. Don't go global to save money. You won't. Salaries in low cost countries may be a bit lower at first, but

not for long. A good researcher in Shanghai, Singapore, Seoul, Bangalore can still command a premium, and if you don't pay fair market value, someone else will—and then some. And all your training dollars will go down the drain. Replicating facilities and resources, implementing global IT, and depreciating all the new Capex will more than eat any anticipated savings.

3.   Don't run global labs as satellites. Give unique, critical path assignments to the teams, and cut the cords with the parent. Everyone needs to be on the hook for something important to the business.

4.   The impact will take much longer than you would like or expect.

Knowledge and experience cannot be quickly imparted. Give yourself at least three years to build momentum and critical mass.

5.   I don't have a magic bullet to prevent loss of intellectual property.

The best approach is to hire intrinsically good people, and nurture them to want to stay and grow with you. And talk to them frequently about the importance of them guarding your secrets, and especially your customers' and suppliers' secrets, even after they leave. And if someone does steal your technology, take your lumps and know that it is part of the added cost of doing business outside of the US, but that in the long run, you simply must be there or you will have no business.

6.   When you encounter fears that HQ is moving jobs to Asia, there is no sugarcoating the fact that, if you don't, your competition will, and then everyone will lose their jobs, so it is better to retain many, but not all, jobs than to lose them all. And that great, highly engaged employees who are smart and work hard and add lots of value to the organization will always have a home.

Chapter Twenty-three
Productivity in R&D

I mentioned in the last chapter that we had built and operated four new global labs with not much change in headcount, and without paying rock-bottom salaries, and still we kept our budget flat for years and years. And all this with increased salaries and benefits from inflation. How? Smoke and mirrors?

The key is R&D productivity. By this, I mean doing more with less. I am not being glib here—it is really important.

The worst thing you can do in R&D is work on a bad project or do a bad experiment. No matter the outcome, you are wasting money. When I first got to CMC, we were pouring money down the drain working on dumb things in dumb ways. For example, we were spending over ten million dollars just on silicon test wafers—the things that chips are grown on. These wafers were eight inch in diameter, less than a sixteenth of an inch thick, and looked like the Jolly Green Giant's pocket change. Whenever we developed a new polishing compound, we would buy dozens of these wafers and polish them, then measure how well we did.

Some of these silicon wafers came a pure coating, for example with tungsten or copper or silicon nitride—typical materials that need to be polished by our customers. These sold for less than a hundred dollars each. But if your experiment required that you polish two hundred of them, you were still looking at twenty thousand dollars for one experiment.

Some of the wafers were patterned with chip-like structures that looked like wires, insulators, gates, transistors—things that you might actually encounter in a real chip. These special patterned test wafers cost a few hundred dollars apiece. Then just as I was getting started, the industry changed from eight-inch-diameter wafers to twelve-inch-diameter wafers, and some of these cost well over a thousand dollas each. Wow. Now do an experiment polishing a hundred at a time. Not chump change.

You can imagine that if you did a bad experiment, you would waste hundreds of thousands of dollars, plus time and opportunity costs. It became incumbent to make sure we did high quality experiments that taught us as much as possible.

Fortunately, there is a system that ensures a systematic process for developing new and improved products in the most efficient way—"six sigma." I was a strong advocate of six sigma as you've already heard from Chapter Nine, having gone through years of training at GE. When I first arrived at CMC, one of our customers was demanding that we use six sigma methods to develop and produce their products. I just took it to the next stage—insisting that everyone use six sigma methods. We quickly had the entire R&D staff trained in experimental design and gage repeatability and reproducibility to make sure our test methods were good enough—often they weren't. Why make a measurement that is unreliable?

By designing better experiments, learning more per experiment, and working with Sourcing and our suppliers to reduce our wafer costs, we were able to cut our wafer budget by more than half, while simultaneously learning more per experiment.

I will tell you that these are tough, tough tests to perform reliably. There was so much variation in materials, process, and measurement, that it was impossible to perform even what I would call a good experiment. But at least we went from an abysmal waste of money, to something akin to our customer's actual process—at least revealing semiquantitative trends in how our products would actually perform in our customer's operations.

I also established a productivity czar who oversaw each of the groups' costs to look for ways to cut without sacrificing results or mission. And in addition to specific cost-cutting projects, each of my direct- reports was given a hundred-thousand dollar annual cost challenge. Just by keeping an eye on costs, we were able to cut them by two to four million dollars a year, year in and year out, which offset most of our inflation and increased globalization expenses. I was quick to provide big cash rewards for people who found savings. And other than a establishing a permanent cost-cutting psyche, I don't feel we ever cut into the meat of what we were trying to do—which was to move the needle forward on CMP technology for our customers.

As I mentioned earlier, every year I would go into our annual marathon budgeting sessions with the 'ogres' from Finance. They would present me with an unthinkable budget target, and each year I would suggest they cut it substantially further. And together, we would go line item by line item, and still find lots of fat. Sure my staff would scream that they needed the fat, but somehow, we always made our budgets by the end of the year, no sweat. Finance and I adored each other, which is how it should be—a true partnership rather than a suspicious overlord protecting the company's cash from spendthrifts.

And on occasion, something new and big would arise mid-year that would cost a lot more than we anticipated. At that point, I would go to Finance and say, "I need X number of dollars to do this new thing," and because they knew how much I cared about managing costs, it was never a problem to get their support if it was possible. You know, my attitude about saving money is that, we are all in business together to make money. Of course saving money is important to me, and doing my projects does not necessarily take precedence. I want to do it all— to save money and get everything done.

And my teams never ran out of ways to save.

Lessons Learned

1. Your company is in business to make money. Cutting waste is a big way to help. There is the occasional waste, and then there is systemic

waste. Doing bad experiments will destroy your budget. Making bad measurements will destroy your budget. Working on bad projects will destroy your budget. Do the things the right way; it usually doesn't cost more.

2.   If you make saving money part of everyone's responsibility, they will deliver, often painlessly. It can even be fun.

3.   Finance and R&D are on the same team. We all want the company to succeed, financially. Working together is the best way to achieve everyone's goals.

4.   I know in some circles, 'six sigma' is a dirty word. I don't think six sigma is a panacea, nor does it replace original and creative thought. It has been poorly taught, preached and forced down people's throats, and has even replaced religion in some people. No wonder folks resent it. But it doesn't have to be that way. For developing new and improved products and processes, it is great. Six sigma makes sure that experiments are efficiently designed and rigorously executed, and that data-driven decisions are made. Six sigma ensures that the customer's needs are paramount. And that the products can be reliably manufactured with high quality and yield. What's bad about that?

Chapter Twenty-four

We Came, We Sawed,
We Were Conquered

Like most businesses, Cabot Microelectronics was always on the lookout for new avenues to growth. Our core polishing business was solid, we had cash in the bank, and were interested in growing either in our core or via adjacencies.

As soon as I arrived at CMC, I started asking the question, "What else can we polish besides chips that will create enormous value?" In short order, we thought of dozens of possible applications including optics, medical devices, tools, heat sinks, and numerous others. As a result of this mental exercise, as a company, we decided to pursue this adjacency, and called the business "ESF" for engineered surface finish.

Several years later, I would call our results mixed. We made two acquisitions, developed some homegrown technologies, got some sales and growth, but achieved nowhere near what I dreamed was possible.

Because this is still a current and ongoing activity for CMC, I can't really comment about the ESF business since so much remains proprietary. On the other hand, I feel it is OK to discuss one last failed effort, since it is equally illustrative as some the others from my more ancient past that we read about in earlier chapters.

Solar energy was really booming the last several years, and we wondered how to enter this segment. Solar cells often use polycrystalline silicon wafers to capture the sun's rays and turn them into electricity by employing the photoelectric effect. But the wafers aren't polished, merely sliced. Rats! We make polishing compounds.

One of our guys did have a thought: the way the wafers are sliced uses a slurry of particles and chemicals, something like the slurries we used for CMP polishing of semiconductors. Why don't we try to make a new, improved version of the cutting slurries? We decided to take it on as a project.

The way that the polycrystalline silicon blocks (ingots) are sliced employs something called a wire saw. Imagine a miles long steel wire that gets wrapped around two pulleys that are spaced a couple feet apart. The wires are pulled taught, wrapped not once, but looped around and around. And each pulley has a series of evenly spaced grooves that the wire sits in. Looked at from the top, the wires are just a series of dozens of evenly spaced parallel lines. The pulleys are turned very fast such that the wire speed is tens of miles per hour.

At the start of the saw is a large reel of wire, and at the end is another large take-up reel. You run the pulleys until the wire from the starting spool is about to run out, and the collection spool is full. And then, if you need to, you can switch directions and run it in reverse so that the collection spool becomes the starting spool and the starting spool now becomes the collection spool.

Now you take the entire set of wires and you cover it with slurry of silicon carbide abrasive that is mixed into an organic liquid- ethylene glycol. This forms a viscous gray suspension that looks like mud, and it tends to stick to the wires. Now you place the ingot of polycrystalline silicon on top of the moving wires and gradually push it downward. The effect of sliding wires coated with the abrasive mud slowly cuts into the block and after a few hours of continuous motion, the mud and wires cut through the entire block into a series of parallel wafers.

The abrasive is rather expensive, and gets recirculated during the cut. Afterward, it is cleaned up and reused, after being blended with some virgin abrasive to make up for losses. It sounds simple, but it is actually a rather advanced and sophisticated technology.

The main reason that so much of the costly abrasive is lost is that it gets caked up with the silicon bits that gets cut out of the silicon ingot. We call that kerf, and it is kind of like the sawdust that would come off of a wood saw. The silicon kerf sticks to the silicon carbide abrasive, reducing its effectiveness.

We had the great idea that if you used water instead of ethylene glycol to suspend the abrasive, a lot of good things could happen. Of course, water is cheaper, safer, and more environmentally acceptable than ethylene glycol, so this would be a savings. And unlike in ethylene glycol, in water, the silicon kerf would not stick to the silicon carbide, so that the recycle efficiency might approach nearly 100% instead of 80% and we might even be able to recover and reuse the silicon kerf, to boot. And we also thought that we could get better cutting speed, reduced power, and more perfect cuts with fewer wire breaks. We also thought we would be able to use thinner wires and finer abrasives which would get more and thinner wafers from the cut—all big drivers of the process economics.

And by and large, we were able to achieve all of these targets. It sounds like a sure winner and we had some motivated customers anxious to give it a try.

How could a project with so many benefits fail?

If you'll pardon the pun, this was a situation of "death by a thousand cuts." In the course of developing and testing this new cutting fluid, we encountered literally dozens of small, niggling issues that needed to be addressed in order to pop our slurry into an existing process and tool. For example, the ethylene glycol doesn't evaporate, but water does. So during the polish, we needed to add some fresh water to make up for the evaporation losses. No big deal, but someone needed to figure out how, and how much water needed to be added. That was just a small speed bump. Also, because the water dried and the ethylene glycol didn't, dried abrasive would collect in various places. No big deal, but someone needed to spray it down with water from time to time to keep the unit clean and functioning. Not a showstopper, but a hassle.

The viscosity of water-based slurries is lower than that of ethylene glycol slurries, so we needed to identify a thickener. There are several thickeners for water, and the one we initially chose had the problem of shear- thinning— the faster you cut, the thinner it got. So we had to fix that, and we did. But our next version of thickener actually degraded permanently over time, so we had to get yet another version of thickener. Such is a day in the life of a new project like ours.

A very serious issue came about from hydrogen generation. Once the waste was collected, which consisted of fine silicon particles in water, ever so slowly, the silicon would react with the water to evolve small amounts of hydrogen-- probably nothing to worry about, but we worried anyway about the risk of explosion. And we solved that problem by adding inhibitors to the system. But all that took time and effort.

Sometimes the wires would jump out of their tracks on the pullies. And for some reason, wire jump was worse in water than in glycol. That was another problem that took time to solve.

If a wire breaks, this is a serious issue for the saw. Luckily, wires were less likely to break with the water-based system. But unfortunately, the wire-break sensor had been developed for a glycol solution, and it didn't work in water because of water's electrical conductivity- yet another problem to solve. Talk about job security!

The ingots were mounted in an epoxy that would hold the sliced wafers together so that they wouldn't fall and break after the cutting was completed. I bet you aren't surprised that the epoxy was stable in glycol, but didn't hold in water. OK need to find a new epoxy that was more water-stable…no problem, just took a few weeks.

Every time we visited a customer with a solution to yesterday's problem, we encountered tomorrow's new problem. And no one issue was serious enough to be a show-stopper—more an annoyance that required an engineering solution, rather than a major invention. And yet, the issues just kept coming and coming. Our customers were beginning to lose patience, simply wanting a complete drop-in substitution that required no process changes—something which we didn't yet have. And after a couple years of encountering, and overcoming literally dozens of issues like the ones I noted above, both our customers and our management lost patience.

Were we about to encounter the last issue, or were there still dozens or hundreds remaining? Its kind of like trying to decide whether to repair or replace your old clunker car. Is the next repair the last one, or is it just the beginning of a new series of unending visits to the repair shop? For the wire saw project, nobody will ever know, I'm afraid. And so, despite enormous progress and potential benefits, a technology was shelved and the project was killed.

Lessons Learned

1. When customers want a drop in substitution, they have little patience for any changes they might need to make in their process, however small the changes and however large the benefits. Change is hard enough, and there really are never any perfect drop-ins, but too many changes can really doom a project.

2. It is always very difficult decision to kill a project, because you never really know how close you are to a final solution. It is important for the project leaders to manage expectations. If a customer, or the brass, has the false expectation that the product is ready to go, they are especially disappointed when there are delays. On the other hand, if you sandbag and give your team forever to solve all the issues, nobody will support the project in the first place. Generally at the start of a project, everyone is extremely optimistic, and they fail to think of all the possible complicating issues that inevitably occur in the real application. As a result, frustration and disillusionment set in and in the extreme, the project is killed.

3.   In general, the more novel the development, the more likely you are to encounter unanticipated issues.

4.   Sometimes, it seems that retrofitting an existing system has a lower barrier to entry than designing an entirely new system. In retrospect, had we partnered with a wiresaw manufacturer and recycler to jointly develop entirely new systems, it may have been more effective than trying to gerryrig and shoehorn the new water-based cutting fluid into one designed for glycol.

5.   Remember that for each of these projects, there are dozens of individuals working on them who care a great deal about the outcome, and whose lives, careers, and livelihoods are affected by their projects' successes or failures. Often, the key business leaders are given a great deal of credit for initiating bold new initiatives, and leverage these kudos as steppingstones to advance their careers. Meanwhile, the researchers are left to slog out the serious issues often long after the business leader has been promoted and moved on. It is a frequent source of resentment for the researcher to see their champion abandon their project right at a critical moment in order to get a promotion. And it is especially vital for the research leadership to be their employees' advocate, and to ensure their careers are not damaged when their projects fail. Otherwise, you get a risk-averse culture that refuses to make bold innovations.

Chapter Twenty-five
Closing Thoughts

I hope by now you have some flavor for life in R&D. If you can only remember one thing from this book, it is that bringing a new, improved item to commerce is damnably hard, even though it happens thousands of times a year across various industries. Each time you walk down the aisle of your Home Depot or Walgreens, try to remember that behind every label and package is someone's heart and soul, and that efforts in man-years or decades are behind each product. For every product you see, there are another dozen or hundred that never made it, and those dozens represent effort, investment, disappointment, and shattered careers for countless, nameless, faceless people and organizations.

You will hear researchers boasting about patents and publications. Those are mere paper. Ask them what they have successfully brought to the marketplace—this is the real story.

There are a plethora of ways to fail in R&D, whether by a thousand cuts or one massive big blow. How often our customer told us exactly what they wanted, something they actually believed until we delivered it to them and found out that what they thought they wanted wasn't what they really wanted, after all. Sorry. How often have we met their needs, but created new and unanticipated side issues? How often have we created the best product, but our customers looked askance and bought from their fellow countrymen, classmates, or brothers-in-law instead?

What about delivering the right product at the wrong time—too early, too late?

And despite the myriad of ways to fail, there remains just one way to succeed—to be substantially better than anything out there that came before. How simple and easy a request is that? Just go set a world's record in some product performance—should be easy. How about something simple like the fastest chip, the tastiest prune, the lightest canoe, the shiniest mirror, the longest-burning lamp? Surely that is much easier than say, breaking the record in the long-jump or two hundred butterfly. When will the new lamp get my picture on a Wheaties® box?

I never met a customer who didn't ask me for exactly what he is getting today, only cheaper and faster, smaller or lighter. Oh, but also- please don't change a thing because they can't afford the time or money to requalify.

Rarely does someone ask for a breakthrough—something they don't even know they need until they see it. Oh except for our big bosses —they always ask for a breakthrough- something visionary and unprecedented. And then they reject it because it is outside of our market, or is untested, untried, untrue, too risky, or cannibalizes our existing product line—what Clayton Christiansen called "The Innovator's Dilemma." And then when someone else comes up with it, they complain, "Where were you? How could you let three guys in a garage out-invent you and the millions of dollars we spent on you?"

I have an especially cold place in my heart for commercial experts who ask me to give them an exact copy of what the customer is already buying- a so-called offset or benchmark. Are we really paying you six figures to come up with, "Do exactly what the competition is doing?" Of course our customers ask for that, and the customer is always right. Then when we have it, the customers merely go to their current supplier and ask for concessions, and we get no business, because there are always switching costs, interruptions in their production to requalify, change control documentation, new labels and standard operating procedures to write up and get signatures for. Coming up with cheap copies only works if you are willing to accept razor-thin margins, and we weren't. Worse—all the time we were developing a "me-too," our competitors were developing a leapfrog, and all we did was waste a lot of time and money sustaining their lead. The moment we deliver a "me-too," they spring out of the woodwork with their new and improved "next-generation" and we are back to catching up again.

You have heard me rant about R&D being an easy scapegoat. Most of the enterprise is operating on a very short leash—daily production schedules, day-sales-outstanding, orders, inventories, receivables, logistics. R&D operates with the longest time frame. It is easy to perceive that R&D lives a life of leisure. And it is certain that a business that runs on quarterly earnings will be way out of synch with research that takes years.

It is also the rare company that sustains R&D through thick and thin. Do you think you can stop and restart a research project without a loss in continuity?

A favorite failure mode for organizations is to jam new R&D projects into the pipeline without killing anything or adding resources. During the planning process, we all agree to pursue certain activities, and assign our resources to one hundred-plus per cent, because we obviously don't want anyone sitting around working on "science projects," or waiting for the phone to ring like the Maytag repairman. And yet when new stuff invariably arises outside of the normal planning process, nothing gets taken off the plate. Naturally, the complaint is that R&D should be finishing projects at the same pace as new ones start. Sure, that would be a nice balancing act. Sadly, new projects often start at a pace that is triple or quadruple what can be finished. Everyone is super busy, but nothing gets completed.

Generally, the business leaders set the priorities for R&D, with triage for quality issues taking precedence, followed by productivity/cost reductions, and maybe simple derivative new products of low risk for delivery next quarter. How often we hear, "If we don't do XYZ now, there won't be a next quarter," and the longer term stuff gets pushed aside. Later, the same business leaders complain that the long-term pipeline is dry even after they set the priorities to be short range to begin with. And that R&D is too slow, and never finishes anything. This is the conundrum.

And think of the poor researcher who is working on a longer range, higher risk project. When it comes time for her performance review, it is often, "What has she done for me lately? We reward results and impact around here, not progress on dubious projects. Show me the money." It is the rare organization that appreciates the good miss. After a few misses in a row, the business begins to wonder if this individual no longer deserves a job. And even when the work is successfully completed and the item is ramped and is selling well a few years later, we hear "Why are you rewarding her now, for work she did three years ago? Our performance appraisal system is all about what she did this last year, not her ancient history." Ouch. Has this happened to you? No wonder our folks gravitate to firefighting. In which case you might hear something like, "You are rewarding Johnny for first developing a product that we can't reliably manufacture, and then reward him again for coming in and fixing it? Why didn't he do it right in the first place?" OK why didn't you give us the time to do it right in the first place? Oh yeah, if we had only done a better job anticipating the customer's needs and worked on long-term projects instead of waiting until the last minute, we would have had time to do it right. I forgot. Shame on me.

Sure we can probably whip up a prototype post haste, but can we make it economically and reliably and be sure it works for our customer day in and day out and be sure it doesn't infringe someone's patent? That takes time. You want us to come up with a breakthrough—something substantially better and out-of-this-world? Something that is so good, it will sell itself? If it were that easy, someone else would have already done it. I won't say that all of the easy stuff is done, but in mature industries, face it-- by and large most of the easy stuff has been done. Yes you might occasionally get lucky, like in our Halogen Ultra XL® of Chapter Fifteen, but that is the exception.

I'm not saying that R&D has no accountability. All too often, we did pursue a path less fruitful than the competition, and the other guys won. Or we would be delayed on a project because of changes in priorities, and miss an important window. Maybe our competition was smarter or worked harder, or just got lucky. Maybe we were spread too thinly and our competition was focused on just one customer or one application and could work without distraction. Maybe our competition was willing to take much less profit, which opened avenues of research we wouldn't consider.

Yes in the end, I am accountable for the portfolio. The R&D buck stops here. If I picked the wrong projects, or allowed the business to jam in too many, then *mea culpa*. At least trust me that my intent was pure—only to do that which I felt was in the best interests of the organization both near term and beyond. I have no other agenda.

I'd be lying if I didn't truly believe from the bottom of my heart, after decades in R&D across organizations and industries, that R&D consistently gets the short end of the stick—disproportionately less credit than we deserve for stuff that works, and disproportionately more blame when it doesn't. How can you not feel burned when the salesman wins a BMW Z4 for a product you developed; the same salesman you fought hard to get the project started and the initial prototype into the hands of the customer in the first place; and where you practically made the sale despite of him. I feel there is little empathy and understanding of the minefield we have to traverse to bring something new to the marketplace.

Want a little cheese with that whine, Spiro?

OK now don't get me wrong. Even though I have spent the last couple hundred pages mostly bellyaching about how hard it is in R&D, I am really and truly not bitter about my career. Quite the contrary, like almost every researcher I know, I wouldn't have it any other way. I had tremendous fun and joy and satisfaction. Every day was indescribably interesting and filled with learning and growth and discovery. I really made a difference with people and products and helped make the economy grow and the world a better place. I enjoyed the trust and respect and friendship of colleagues and the community. I got to learn things and see things and do things that were amazing. I got to see atoms under the highest of magnification, I walked inside of factories that were doing astonishing things like making chips with circuits a ten thousandth the diameter of a human hair, CT scanners and MRI imagers that enabled breakthroughs in medical diagnostics and treatments. I saw raw metal coming into one end of a plant, and a locomotive or jet engine come out the other. I travelled around the world fifty times, visiting customers, suppliers, partners, and attending conferences and courses. I saw wild elephants and monkeys, the Eiffel Tower, Stonehenge, the Great Wall, the Emperor's Palace, the back streets of Hong Kong and the skyline of Singapore at night. It has been a glorious, glorious career and a great life and I am so grateful for it.

And oh yes, I got paid very well, thank you very much.

So sure, we in R&D have been frustrated by a lack of understanding from our colleagues—which is why I had to write this book. God knows the folks in Sales and Finance and Operations are just as frustrated about us folks in R&D as we are about them. But in the end, we all really are on the same team with the same hopes for our customers to succeed and be delighted by buying and using our products and services.

My main hope in writing this book is that now, you might better understand what R&D is really like in the trenches, and maybe have just a teensy bit more empathy toward the white-coats down the hall and understand why they are scowling at you from time to time.

Finally, the marketplace is a cruel mistress, but she never lies. If you have developed an item of commerce or put a new process into a factory, you are my hero. So many jobs and measures are highly subjective. But if you created and delivered something people actually buy- you have undeniably made an important contribution to the world. The marketplace rarely rewards second best.

Let us never forget Trotsky's adage that we are "three square meals from a revolution." Any economy in a tailspin is at risk, along with its underlying government and constitution. The only sustainable economy is one that continuously grows through innovation and its resultant productivity. If it wasn't for us nerds, there would be no innovation, no productivity, no growth—just the inevitable decline and fall of the empire.

Thomas Friedman told us in "The World Is Flat," that globalization is the great economic leveler, and that the only way that today's economic leaders can sustain their peoples' lifestyles is through innovation—the kind that creates enormous value and productivity. No pressure, folks, but if you are in R&D, you have the weight of the free world on your shoulders. Enjoy and Godspeed to you. You'll need all the help you can get!

About the Author

Cliff Spiro grew up in Willoughby, Ohio. He attended Stanford University, earning in 1976, a BS degree with honors in Chemistry. In 1980, Spiro received a PhD in Chemistry from Caltech where he shared the McCoy prize for the top thesis. He joined GE's Corporate Research and Development in 1980, spending the next twenty plus years with GE in a series of progressively responsible research and leadership positions. In 2001, Cliff left GE to become VP of R&D at Nalco, the industrial water, paper, and energy subsidiary of the French multinational, Suez. In 2003, Spiro became VP of R&D at Cabot Microelectronics where he served until 2011. In 2011, Cliff started the Cliff Spiro Consulting Group, with emphasis on coaching and growing innovation leadership. Spiro also served on the Boards of Directors of Maxdem, inc. of Duarte, CA, The Mississippi Polymer Technologies Corporation of Bay Saint Louis, MS, and Strategic Diagnostics of Newark, DE. Spiro also served on academic boards at The University of Chicago, Northwestern University, and the University of Arizona. He holds twenty US patents and has published extensively in international journals and conferences.

Cliff has two grown children, Ian and Miranda, and lives with his partner, Linda, in Savannah, GA.

Made in the USA
San Bernardino, CA
16 June 2013